The Fashioned Self

JOANNE FINKELSTEIN

Polity Press

First published 1991 by Polity Press in association with Basil Blackwell

Editorial office:
Polity Press, 65 Bridge Street,
Cambridge CB2 1UR, UK

Marketing and production:
Basil Blackwell Ltd
108 Cowley Road, Oxford OX4 1JF, UK

ISBN 0 7456 0687 3

British Library Cataloguing in Publication Data
Finkelstein, Joanne
  The fashioned self.
  1. Self – Sociological perspectives
  I. Title
  302.54

Typeset in 11 on 13 pt Garamond
by Graphicraft Typesetters Ltd Hong Kong
Printed in Great Britain by T.J. Press, Padstow, Cornwall

The Fashioned Self

Contents

Introduction

It is only shallow people who do not judge by appearances. The true mystery of the world is the visible, not the invisible.

Oscar Wilde, *The Picture of Dorian Gray*

In the late twentieth century, our tacit understanding of human character seems to be derived from a motley assemblage of contradictory ideas. On the one hand, we hastily read character physiognomically, from the shape of the individual's nose and chin, or the colour of the eyes and hair; on the other, we create a sense of identity by dressing or behaving after a particular fashion or style. We know, too, that other people, in all likelihood, are doing the same. They may be wearing a hair piece, using hair dye or displaying a sun-tan or have had plastic surgery or a hair transplant. We know that appearances are created and that dressing after a particular fashion is done in order to convey a certain impression. It would seem that the ideas we hold about personal identity, incorporating as they do these divergent views, suggest that our knowledge of human character and our speculations about the nature of our own consciousness and that of others are incoherent and unsystematized narratives, interwoven with contradictory ideas and assumptions. How we arrived at this point and what consequences it has for our contemporary social relations in the societies of the industrialized West is the focus of this book.

1

Introduction

In the consumer culture of modern society, physical appearance has come to be seen as an important means for claiming a degree of social status. High fashion and designer styles in clothing, individualized fitness programmes, exercise equipment for home use, private gymnasiums, diet regimens and cosmetic surgery are readily available as the means for perfecting our physical appearance. The pervasiveness of these goods and services indicates an ethos in which physical appearance is held to be of paramount importance. Indeed, appearance is often conflated with the more spiritual or abstract qualities of character: people are described as having a kind, honest, determined or gentle face as if this expresses their real character.

This conflation of reality with appearance has a long tradition. Sennett's (1976) historical account of the emergence of the modern sensibility vividly detailed the process by which the enactment or the performance of certain emotions and personality traits became the demonstrable proof of their actual existence. The individual was as s/he appeared to be, the suit of clothes, for example, did reveal character; hence, the stylization of appearance became an important focus of the interpersonal or social encounter. The same conflation of appearance with reality is found in the history of Western painting. The female face has been painted for hundreds of years as if it were artificial and masklike (Ribeiro 1987). The sixteenth-century face had an enamelled look. It was glazed over with an egg-white after being coated with ceruse, a lead base paint which gave a hard white appearance. To contrast with this deadly, harsh whiteness, vivid blobs of red were painted on the cheeks. These cosmetics had a poisonous lead content and their deleterious effects were quite marked; however, the portraiture of the times did not reveal this. The seventeenth-century fashions in appearance continued with these harsh cosmetics while, all the time, representing the fashionable sitters for these paintings as being natural beauties. As fashions changed and the enamelled mask of the female face gave way to a less controlled appearance in the eighteenth and nineteenth centuries, the reliance on cosmetics to bring about an attractive appearance did not diminish. In reality, particularly before the nineteenth century, the effects of a deficient diet, infrequent washing and illnesses

2

such as smallpox could be seen in the face where the skin was pitted and blemished by eczema, scurvy and so on. A general ignorance of dental hygiene and the widespread consumption of sugar also meant that tooth decay frequently marred a good face. The painted image showed none of these signs.

It has been common practice, especially in the upper classes, to employ a variety of cosmetics and devices to alter appearance. For instance, cloth or silk patches were employed to cover skin blemishes, wigs were used to give the luxuriance of curly hair and plumpers of cork, wax or leather were used to replace a lost tooth and round out the cheeks (Ribeiro 1987). In some instances, these techniques acquired other uses; for example, in the French courts face patches were cut into various shapes such as stars, hearts and moons, and transposed into a code that no longer concealed pustules but spoke of sexual intrigues.

While techniques for styling appearances have radically altered over the centuries, they are, nonetheless, as popular in contemporary society as in any previous time; indeed, the availability of goods and services has meant that the fashioning of appearances is probably greater in the twentieth century. This suggests that the perceptual conspiracy which allows the artificial complexion and body shape to be seen as a natural representation of character, and the fashioned styles of beauty to be accepted as expressions of human sensibility, remains as convincing as ever.

Blurring the distinctions between the image and reality by emphasizing appearances has a substantial influence on how we see one another. When we value physical appearance as a means of increasing our success or effectiveness in social interactions, we risk limiting the social experience to a barter or exchange controlled by prevailing stereotypes. For instance, when the assumption is widely held that character is integral to appearance and appearances determine the manner of conduct, then the stereotypes of the jolly fat person, the thin anxious person, the dark-complexioned, untrustworthy person, the fair-haired, open-faced, frank person become the currency of sociality. On the strength of these stereotypes, if we are able to train ourselves to make more detailed observations of others' physical attributes, we can come to believe we are making an astute reading of their personalities. Within this framework, understanding human character becomes a matter of perception: the tell-tale detail, the odd combination of this with that, the daring use of colour, texture, size and so on, would be the signs from which we deduce the other's essential self.

How we interpret these signs of character is culturally contingent. What we find aesthetic and attractive about the human body and physical appearance is not determined by nature or any overarching biological principle; our views are not emanations of a universal nature. Rather, our reading of the body is subject to the influences of circumstances; thus the body itself is a contingency which can be made aesthetic or fashioned in accord with prevailing customs. As our evaluations of the body are refracted through the social order, what constitutes the normal physical body – what is physical beauty, what is abhorrent and not acceptable, what immediately repulses us or, conversely, ignites our passions – are ideas and attitudes which are historically and culturally contingent. Régnier-Bohler (1988: 359) has described the medieval individual with a clear complexion as being attributed with a sanguine personality and the dark-skinned individual as saturnine and melancholic. Realizing the cultural and historical contingency of these interpretations should determine that any insight into an essential self which we derive from reading the outward signs is better understood as a reading of a cultural moment than it is an analysis of personality. Yet, this is not often the case.

In industrialized, high technology societies, we have become confident that most of our imagined needs and desires can be translated into material form. We are accustomed to exerting power over our environment and manufacturing all manner of objects to meet our desires. In such a society, the human body, as if no different from other manufactured objects, can be used as a commodity to display power, prestige and status. Like the purchased object, the body can be made a sign of the individual's accomplishments, talents, capacities and character. The early social theorists, Veblen (1899) and Simmel (1904), both recognized how the characteristics of a burgeoning consumer-oriented culture could be promulgated through attitudes toward the human body. The manner of adornment and the use of the body as a means for conspicuous consumption, say, in the pursuit of leisure activities, or in the display of exclusive and exotic goods, established the practices of conspicuous consumption as effective ways of widely displaying personal characteristics. Thus, the shaping and adorning of the body has become a way for the individual to present his or her desired self-image to others.

In a culture where the possession and control of goods and services are highly valued, transforming the body into a commodity which can be used for the display of coveted items becomes a social goal in itself. In the modern era we treat the body as malleable and have developed the tools by which it can be continuously altered in appearance. Clothes, diet, exercise, pharmaceuticals, drug therapy, micro-surgery, body implants and so on, are the means of producing the modern fashioned body. As long as physical appearance remains of singular importance to our social activities, the cosmetic, health and therapeutic industries are assured of retaining their lucrative businesses.

What does it say of our understanding of identity or human character that we have fused together the capacity for conspicuous consumption with the presentation of personality? What does it say of us that we readily accept appearances and habits of conduct as revelations of the private self? What does it say of our social relations that we frequently employ a fashioned self-image and a style of acting in order to create a certain impression through which we hope to influence the opinions others have of us or how they will act toward us?

The nineteenth century was a period in which appearance and the reading of character from physical features was immensely popular. A physiognomist of the day, Samuel Wells, described the process of how to read character.

> We instinctively, as it were, judge the qualities of things by their outward forms. 'Appearances' are said to be 'often deceitful'. They are sometimes seemingly so; but in most cases, if not in all, it is our observation that is in fault. We have but to look

again, and more closely and carefully, to pierce the disguise, when the thing will appear to be just what it is. Appearances do not often deceive the intelligent observer.

A strong association between human character and physical appearance would mean that personality was available to us from the details and displays of personal affectations. It is as if the interior qualities of the individual, the essential self, were being exhibited through the contours of appearance. So, to accept that character is immanent in appearance is tantamount to saying we need only observe certain features in the other and we will know his or her character. This assumes, in effect, that there is a subterranean psychology of human character which is capable of being embodied in the material – either in objects or patterns of generic conduct. But, reading character from outward signs reduces the need to ruminate over our impressions or to review their accuracy. If we accept that human character is immanent in appearance, the need to think about the dynamics of social life becomes superfluous.

Intuitively, we, in the modern consumer-oriented culture, respond to this viewpoint that character is immanent in appearance with scepticism. After all, it is commonly the case that we change our opinions of others, we puzzle over their conduct and then reject our first impressions. Furthermore, too much emphasis is placed on our social skills and knowledge of interaction rituals for us to think them unimportant in our human affairs. In the light of these emphases, it cannot be said that appearances are ultimately so important. But even with this in mind, it is apparent that we are inclined to read character from physical appearances, although, not always to admit to doing so. Certainly, the belief in the power of appearance to reveal character gives the pastime credence, and it would be foolish as Oscar Wilde has stated above to ignore the signs before us. Physical features such as colouring, height, weight, agility and prowess have been translated into a modern parlance which defines attractiveness, sex appeal, emotionality, sobriety, virtue and so on. Being in possession of distinct physical qualities is frequently interpreted as a sign of an archetypical character or disposition, and when such attributes go against the grain of convention, then one risks becoming a social pariah.

In our everyday commerce it would seem that we moderns accept that appearances matter without probing into why they should. The physiognomists, in particular, regarded physical appearance as the key to understanding human character, and over the centuries, they mapped human physical features; they systematically typified which nose shape, what angle of the jaw, size of eyes and colour of hair, were indicative of specific human characteristics. To read the physiognomists in the late twentieth century, and learn which facial feature reveals a propensity toward greed or ambition or unreliability may strike us as quaint and relatively useless in comparison with our modern, rigorous techniques for reading human capabilities and potentials. On the other hand, when we do encounter individuals with striking or anomalous physical appearances, say, they are unusually tall, have a strong body odour, perhaps, they blush irrepressibly, stutter in their speech or have uncontrolled body twitches, in short, when our social relations with another become so infested with obvious physiological signs that we cannot see beyond them, then the endurance of the physiognomic perspective into the modern world seems unassailable. It seems that the more obvious the physical trait, the more willing we are to read the other's character from it. As it is through our public conduct that much of our self-image is presented to others, when the social encounter is dominated by appearances and the mannerisms of the physical body, then our sociality is made more vulnerable to the influences of the received meanings and preconceptions of our times.

To accept, in the twentieth century, that character is summarized in our bodies, that personality and individuality are a function of our appearance and physical prowess, confronts us, to some extent, as an unlikely article of faith. Yet, when we consider the popularity of practices such as cosmetic surgery, strenuous exercise and dieting, which transform our body shape and appearance and which are frequently undertaken on the belief that our sense of self will be more assured when our appearance is different, then we are forced to consider that a continuity of thought with that of the physiognomists may be being expressed. Why else, we must ask ourselves, is there a proliferation of commercially available and therapeutically endorsed strategies and techniques regularly advertised in the mass media which promise to produce a new self and transform the old? Why is so much time and money spent on the shaping of our physical appearance, and how is it that the industries succoured by these efforts, such as the fashion, cosmetic and health industries, are so successful? We may decline to endorse the view that we judge by appearances because it seems such a superficial and inherently unjust idea, but, at the same time, it is apparent that we do so.

Heller (1989) has pointed out that the authenticating narratives employed to explain our times are not necessarily grounded in facticity. Some ideas gain an authority at one level but fail to convince at another. Ideas that go unquestioned in the course of everyday life, and which exist as self-evident truths, may not pass as real or true on a more abstract philosophical or intellectual level. These ideas are myths; in their everyday usage they do not reveal themselves as such, nor do they suggest that there are different ways of looking, that there are differences in kinds of knowledge, differences between fact, interpretation and fiction; instead, they appear as if true. The ways in which we currently understand personal identity or character illustrate the point. Our present views on identity are grounded in the ambiguous principles of physiognomy and other unexamined assumptions of human nature. These ideas, which work as authenticating narratives of the modern age, give a sense of facticity to various patterns of perception and habits of conduct. Yet, such narratives are authoritative without necessarily being factual, and in the following chapters of this book, this is illustrated with an account of the endurance of the physiognomic perspective into the modern era.

The physiognomic perspective is found in contemporary attitudes toward physical appearance, especially those which legitimate the deliberate reshaping of the body to approximate prevailing norms. Where a reliance on physical appearances as an expression of character can be seen to exist, opportunities are created for fictive portrayals of the self in which individuals can be spuriously assigned or claim for themselves a wealth of virtues. Understanding human character from appearances, styles and images is an authoritative narrative of modern social life which has a significant influence on our habits of sociality. For instance, individuals who have physically groomed themselves in accord with prevailing definitions of beauty and attractiveness can feel confident of having constructed for themselves an appropriate and successful social identity. Such individuals have absorbed the prevailing values and have produced a social demeanour and sense of identity which will successfully carry them through the everyday world. Yet, the sense of self enjoyed by these individuals is, ironically, constituted from the received meanings of the times. That is, their sense of self is an embodiment of the representational fiction of a self. This sense of identity is a concatenation of prevailing ideas, yet it is experienced as unique because these elements and ideas have been idiosyncratically arranged by circumstances. Such a self can be said to be accidental (see Heller 1989).

Using the idea of the self as an authenticating narrative of the times is not equivalent to saying that personality is an imposed, uniform, pre-figured or structured phenomenon. The individual's sense of self has not been perfectly absorbed from the external; unique biographical circumstances have differentiated each individual to a great extent. In our acting in accord with prevailing meanings we come to think of ourselves as being in possession of a personality or character. This belief does not constitute a realm of subjectivity, nor do our unique circumstances constitute a self or sense of personal identity. Importantly, the authenticating narrative which determines that there is an entity known as the self is itself a repository of the received meanings of the times. Thus, the narrative which authenticates the self tells us that we are in possession of a character, a personal identity, a putative reservoir of subjective experience merely because we act in the world. The consequence of such a narrative is that it authenticates a self-centred self.

Such a sense of self works well enough at the prosaic level of daily social intercourse but when the constituents of the self are called for, we find ourselves speaking through clichés, platitudes and received meanings. The authenticating narrative that we have condensed into character reveals a self that is a representational synthesis of contingencies. This is vividly illustrated through our commonsense belief that character can be thought of as immanent in appearance and that human physiognomy can reveal a great deal of the individual's character.

Physiognomy may be considered a discarded intellectual relic from our pre-scientific days yet, on examination, it can be seen operating in contemporary society, albeit rewritten into a modern form. The tenets of physiognomy are not factual, neither are they systematic nor consistent, rather, they have been modified by many proponents over many centuries. Some physiognomic perspectives maintained that there was an essential or given self which emanated through certain physical features. This meant that human character was a fully formed 'interior' and unmodifiable by experience. Other perspectives did not completely overlook the influence that circumstances may have on the individual, and proponents of these insisted that human character could be altered by experiences. This latter approach regarded character more as a summation of both interior predispositions and external influences.

The kernel of the physiognomic perspective was that the physical appearance of the individual reflected much of his or her character. Physiognomy viewed human character as immanent in appearance, yet it could absorb into its paradigm the human desire to fashion, adorn, emphasize and refashion the body. After all, whether appearances were inherited or cultivated, the value of appearance was unequivocal, and the chthonic belief remained that appearances were telling summaries of personal character. Fashioning or cultivating an appearance was merely the opportunity to realize the self more fully by maximizing the virtues suggested by physical attributes. So, in the physiognomic view, hair colour, the size of eyes, ears, nose and chin, the mobility of the mouth and lips, the height of the forehead, the shape of the face and the presence of wrinkles, could all be taken as signs of the self, irrespective of whether these were natural formations or had been deliberately styled and shaped.

At first glance, it would seem that we moderns would not

accept the physiognomic idea that character is an inherent quality embedded within us and revealed through appearance; we are more inclined to see ourselves as self-produced, the result of our own efforts, desires and interests. And yet, in our strong interest in appearance and our deliberate attempts to fashion and shape the body, we have tacitly endorsed the essential idea of the physiognomic perspective that the image and appearance of the individual is somehow representative of character and sensibility. In so doing, we have created the opportunity for bestowing upon individuals a host of spurious virtues and vices.

It is the value accorded the image, above all else, which carries the ancient physiognomic perspective into the modern era, even though, at the same time, we recognize that linking self-identity with physical appearance produces a myriad of anomalies. For example, what does it suggest of the individual's character when s/he possesses an unconventional body which does not demonstrate the usual standards of mobility, dexterity and proportion? Are those individuals with spina bifida, cerebral palsy or Down's syndrome of flawed character and irreversibly different from others? Does the acquisition of a slow degenerative disease like Parkinson's or Alzheimer's bring about a change in essential character? If so, this would present an anomaly in the physiognomic system. By the same token, we could ask whether the owners of anarchic bodies also become the embodiments of unconventional identities? Furthermore, what sense can be made of conduct which is self-polluting, for example, when individuals regularly imbibe too much alcohol or consume too many calories? Are these instances of an individual in possession of a rebellious body, and by implication, a rebellious character?

Regarding the physical body as being the repository of character and as having a life of its own which can emanate into the social situation and influence the nature of our social relations is not the way we commonly think of the self. At the same time, though, there are numerous circumstances where we do regard the body as capable of independence as if it could act against us, be a liability, even betray character, such as when it

Introduction

succumbs to illness (Sontag 1977) or shows signs of self-abuse or a disturbed self-image as in cases of anorexia nervosa (Bruch 1978).

It would seem, then, that a reading of human character through an interpretation of bodily signs, while a common practice, is thoroughly confused. The knowledge of self and identity that may result from these speculations is replete with anomalies. Yet, it is paradoxical that in the high regard we have for the way we look, we are accepting this narrative as if it were true. To this extent, we cannot claim to be any more sophisticated in our understanding of human character than those in previous eras who interpreted it through the pseudo-sciences of physiognomy, chiromancy, phrenology and astrology. Indeed, the present popularity of astrology and our frequent reliance upon physiognomic interpretations of bodily characteristics indicate that examples of unsubstantiated pseudo-scientific ideas, some of which are quite remote from any principles of orthodoxy, are still widely held (Wrobel 1988). When we blithely apply such ideas to the conduct of our social lives, we, in the late twentieth century, may well be as gullible and as conceptually jejune as any generation before us. It is the argument of this book that as long as we continue to value physical appearances, and sustain the enormous industries which trade on this value, namely, the consumer-oriented cosmetic, fashion and therapeutic industries, we authenticate a narrative of human character which is spurious. Furthermore, by sustaining an emphasis on image and appearances, we prevent the emergence of a narrative which would give birth to a capacity for reflexivity and subjectivity, and a sense of self in which universal rather than narrow and contingent values were predominant.

Finally, a word on how the argument has been presented. The book is divided into three sections: the first, consisting of chapters 1 and 2, explores the physiognomic view and illustrates how its tenets have instructed our contemporary views on the human form; the second section, chapters 3, 4 and 5, describes how the body is fashioned in the contemporary society and how it has been employed as a sign expressive of the

12

individual's self-conception; and the final section, chapters 6 and 7, presents a theoretical exploration of what consequences may apply to the nature of social life when the signs of the self, that is, appearance and a fashioned self-image, are construed as synonymous with character.

Part I
The Physiognomic Body

1

Character as Immanent in Appearance

Systematic accounts of a relationship between physical appearance and human character have appeared throughout Western history. Physiognomy was one such account in which the prognostication of human character was made from the study of physical features. Astrology was another system for reading character; it assumed that the planets influenced the individual's physical and mental capabilities and this was evidenced through body type, colouring, movement and gait. Early accounts of Eastern medicine from the tenth, twelfth and fourteenth centuries included a system of character analysis which combined physiognomy with astrology, and this established, amongst other things, that the forehead corresponded to Mars, 'the right eye to the Sun, the left to Venus, the right ear to Jupiter, the left to Saturn, the nose to the Moon, the mouth to Mercury' (Magli 1989:111). Whole communities could be characterized as Lunar or Mercurial or Saturnine. Lunar people were small-bodied and lively, Mercurial individuals were smaller still, imaginative with subtle and serious interests; they were engaged with writing, astrology and white magic. Those influenced by Saturn were patient, those influenced by Jupiter were prudent, Mars individuals were courageous, and the Sun bestowed wisdom and magnificence upon those under its influence (Magli 1989:111).

I The Physiognomic Body

Although the systems of astrology and physiognomy were thought to be closely intertwined, by the Middle Ages a theory of the temperaments had been absorbed into the formula for reading character largely because individuals were often observed to have physical features which were not consistent with their astrological heritage. The unreliability of the planetary signs as indicators of character meant that more rigour was required in the matter of character analysis, and, eventually, a theory which blended the elements, qualities and humours emerged. This new system could account for a more complex character; thus, 'the man who is irascible not only has the nature of fire, but also that of the lion; the phlegmatic man has both the nature of water and that of the lamb; the sanguine man has both the nature of air and that of the monkey; the melancholic one has the nature of earth and that of the pig' (Magli 1989:105).

From this melting pot of ideas about human character, a hierarchical ordering of physical features slowly evolved which eventually gave prominence to the physiognomic over the astrological reading of physical features. In such a schema, the head came to be designated the principal repository of character traits, so the head's own features, namely, the forehead, hair, eyebrows, eyes, nose, mouth, lips, teeth, chin, ears, face, neck and throat became correspondingly important. Of subsidiary importance were the individual's hands and body. Although, early treatises on physiognomy linked it with astrology, the longest tradition of the idea appears to have descended through Hippocrates, Aristotle and Galen, who, in particular, bequeathed a system of humoural influence that characterized Western medicine for more than a millennium (Pack 1974:113–38).

The most ancient work on physiognomy, the third century BC treatise *De Physiognomonica*, is attributed to Aristotle; however, its authenticity has not been universally admitted. The pseudo-Aristotelian works *Physiognomia* and *Aristotelis philosophi phisnomia* both argued for a relationship between human appearance and temperament by drawing an analogy with animals (Foerster 1893). Thus, the individual's physical approximation to an animal suggested that the character of the

18

individual could be ascertained by analysing the animal. As
animal characteristics were well enough known, then the individual who resembled a bull or an owl or a snake was thought
to be in possession of those same traits. Specifically, those
resembling a lion would be hot-tempered and strong, those
resembling a leopard, would have delicate features but would
also be proud, deceitful, scheming as well as daring and fearful.
The bear was thought deceitful, fierce, irascible as were those
who resembled it. 'The wild boar is full of senseless rage, while
the ox is simple and sincere. The horse likes pomp and craves
honors. The fox is deceitful and scheming; the monkey likes
joking and imitating. Sheep are self-assured; goats are lecher-
ous; pigs are dirty and greedy (and) if a man appears similar to
an animal in any of his features, let him be aware that he shall
behave in a similar fashion' (Magli 1989:101–3). The idea was
that physical appearance was suited to a particular manner of
behaving, so how people looked spoke eloquently of how they
would conduct themselves.

In *De Physiognomonica*, the entire animal world was divided
into two parts, the male and female, and these characteristics
were echoed in humans, so, for instance, the female like the
panther was thought to be treacherous, and the male like the
lion was thought to be bold. As Magli has stated, 'this gives
rise to a long list of character masks: Goat-Man, Lion-Man,
Bird-Man, Monkey-Man' (1989:101). Other influences such as
those from Hippocratic teachings designated the build of the
body as an important sign of character and claimed that the
individual's physical stature was significant as a sign of the
individual's internal disposition, although not as important as
the face.

The use of physiognomy as a system for the analysis of
human character has endured as a popular narrative. Over the
centuries, there have been numerous examples of ancient Greek
and Latin texts expressing these ideas which have been translated and reworked. For example, the Eastern text, *Secreta
Secretorum*, was a tenth- or eleventh-century reworking of the
Aristotelian thesis which had further influence on other works
such as John Metham's fifteenth-century physiognomic essay,
written in English, where he declared 'the most trwe werkyng

off nature ys in a mannys face' (Craig 1915). A twelfth-century
work on facial colouring and complexions by Rasis, written in
Arabic, has been reproduced in modern French by Mourad
(1939). The manuscript *Physionomia Rationalis* is a translation
from the Latin by Claud de la Bellière, a counsellor to the
French king. It used Galen and Aristotle with some biblical
references to prove that the individual's health goes with his or
her appearance. The text, consisting of forty questions, was
translated into English in the seventeenth century by Robert
Baker. In 1586 Giovanni Battista della Porta (1536–1615) published in Venice a physiognomic work, *De Humana Physiognomia*, which analysed the individual's character, appearance
and destiny. Another sixteenth-century text by the prolific
Girolamo Cardano, entitled *Metoposcopia*, was probably available in an abbreviated German translation made in the late
seventeeth-century; Johann Lavater may have used this to establish the modern school of physiognomy. John Spon published
Faces: What They Mean and How to Read Them in 1934, and
claimed that it was a reworking of an earlier sixteenth-century
script which was, in all likelihood, written by della Porta.

The influences of astrology and physiognomy persisted for
centuries alongside humoural theory. Indeed, each of these
strands of thought can be seen in a popular seventeenth-
century book on palmistry and physiognomy written by a
priest, which went to six English editions. This text stated that
when the sun is in Pisces, the individual will have a 'fair
forehead, clear skin, large and fair eyes', and when the sun is in
Leo, the individual will have 'a small, comely body, ruddy
coloured, mixed with white rolling eyes ... and full of diseases
in their feet' (Indagine 1666). In short, the origins and lineage
of the physiognomic perspective are difficult to establish, but it
is enough to recognize that it has been an idea of enduring
appeal which seems to have answered the persistent desire of
members of various societies to explain and make predictions
about the nature of human character.

In the long history of physiognomic reasoning, there are
many different accounts of the ways in which human character
is related to the individual's observable physical features.
Generally, physiognomy has dealt with the uncovering of per-

1 Character as Immanent in Appearance

sonality traits through the study of facial features, body structure and overall physical appearance. It has been assumed that there was an immanent and univocal essence in humans which was reflected through identifiable body parts, even though some parts, such as the face, seemed responsive and often changeable in appearance and quality. Nonetheless, the physiognomists claimed that character could be read from specific features of human appearance, especially those which were immobile – the chin and forehead, for example, were regarded as especially revealing of the individual's potential for aggression. George Turner, writing in 1641 on astronomy and 'astrologic' (*sic*), devoted forty pages to 'phisiognomy'. He had rules by which character could be interpreted from the nose, lips, ears, chin, pitch of the voice, lines on the forehead, movement of the eyes, number of teeth, the size of the tongue and so on. Turner described his work as a collection for his own personal use but which was taken from many authors; thus, it can be regarded as a useful summary of opinions and perspectives prevalent in the mid-seventeenth century. Turner regarded the shape of the nose as the most telling feature; it revealed the individual's cruelty, revengefulness, benevolence and overall degree of aggression, quarrelsomeness and courage (1641:114). A person's ears revealed the degree of intelligence, memory and foolishness (Turner 1641:115); the thickness of the lips indicated how much heat the individual held and, as it was heat which dulled the senses, the thickness of the lips (ibid:116–7, 143) indicated much about the individual. For instance, imbecility was reflected in small, thin lips, courage in an overhanging upper lip, uncleanliness and folly in thick lips with a round mouth. Other signs of character were in the 'overbrows' or eyebrows, hair, hands, nails, shoulders, 'ribbes', neck, throat, beard and laughter. In the case of too much laughter, stupidity was indicated, and a sufficient amount indicated courtesy (Turner 1641:120).

Certain representations of the physiognomic perspective claimed as a fundamental assertion that the human shape and facial features were signs which both foretold and reflected the moral characteristics of the individual. This meant that some features could be interpreted as prognostications of specific character traits. This was an audacious claim because it suggested a behavioural determinism behind an individual's appearance, thereby making it seem that certain traits were secreted in physical attributes and that appearance was the major impetus behind character. For example, according to this type of physiognomic reasoning, the individual with small, black eyes, a receding chin and thin hair would probably become a criminal or degenerate. There were other claims as well which depicted certain physical features as reflective of character after those features had been shaped by experience. Thus, one could tell much of an individual's past from his or her features; certain physical features could act as summaries of the individual's past experiences and, as such, they could inadvertently disclose personality traits. In this sense, one's physical appearance could be a betrayal of one's private self.

It was the eighteenth-century work of Johann Caspar Lavater (1741–1801) which stands out as the most elaborated exposition of physiognomy. His huge, four-volume treatise *Physiognomische Fragmente zur Beförderung der Menschenkenntniss und Menschenliebe* (1775–8) was a systematic presentation of how physical characteristics corresponded with moral traits. The text was copiously illustrated with silhouettes of the human form. It also contained the writings of other thinkers equally enthusiastic about physiognomy, namely, Herder and Goethe. A further detailed work by Lavater, and not published, was *Mélanges de regles Physiognomiques*, prepared in 1793, as a gift to his patron, Eric Magnus de Staël, who was himself celebrated for his own extraordinarily handsome appearance (Marwick 1988).

Lavater's principles of physiognomy enjoyed wide popularity. The novelist Victor Hugo, half a century later, spoke of Lavater as if he were a household name. In *Les Misérables*, Hugo claimed of one of his fictional characters that 'Lavater, if he could have studied this face, would have found in it a mixture of vulture and pettifogger; the bird of prey and the man of tricks rendering each other ugly and complete' (1862:256). The name of Lavater was well known and his system of character analysis widely subscribed to probably because it was so detailed and exact and, thereby, readily understandable. Even though Lavater presented his physiognomic system as a scientific analysis of character, it became a type of parlour game and form of entertainment for the European upper classes of the late eighteenth and early nineteenth centuries. The laws and tenets of physiognomy were often printed on cards, like playing cards, one of which showed an embossed head sectioned off into physiognomically visible attributes. This format allowed easy reference as well as the wide dissemination of the ideas. Having such a set of cards was itself fashionable. Lavater's physiognomy even spawned its own satire in 1778–9, a four-volume work known as *Physiognomical Travels* by a German satirist, Johann Karl August Musäus.

Lavater's claims for physiognomy were grand. He presented it as a total system of analysis; all three elements of the individual, namely, the physiological, intellectual and moral, were analysed in his system; indeed, they were intimately connected with each other and were 'expressed in every part of the body' (1885:10). Physiognomy was, he stated:

the science or knowledge of the correspondence between the external and internal man, the visible superficies (*sic*) and the invisible contents ...
The moral life of man, particularly, reveals itself in the lines, marks, and transitions of the countenance. His moral powers and desires, his irritability, sympathy, and antipathy; his facility of attracting or repelling the objects that surround him; these are all summed up in, and painted upon, his countenance when at rest. (1885:11, 9)

Lavater urged others to see the necessity of physiognomy as a proper mode of social discourse on the basis that everyone was a physiognomist whether they knew it or not. After all, judging others by their outward appearance was a seemingly instinctual law of social life; everyone judged character from 'those first impressions which are made by (the individual's) exterior' (1885:12). One may as well study Lavater's rules and recommendations in order to do it correctly because, he maintained (1885:47), one could always improve one's abilities and acquire new interpretive skills. Although, the natural propensity was to judge others by appearance one could, under

23

tutelage, discipline this practice into a more exact science of character analysis – the benefits of which, Lavater predicted, would be immediately apparent.

Lavater's account of human character was based on the idea that the human body was capable of endless transformations, the face, in particular, showed a panorama of emotions and thoughts, and the body was constantly altering in appearance because of fatigue, excitement, illness and so on. Nonetheless, Lavater regarded the physical appearance of the individual as an accurate summation of moral character. He regarded the face as the most explicit sign of character including the size and shape of the skull, the forehead and the direction of the facial wrinkles. Human beauty proved the inner worth and virtue of the individual and, conversely, ugliness demonstrated vice. Lavater argued further that the moral background of the individual was unequivocally revealed in appearance. Certain characteristics could be inherited, for example, the moral decadence of a family as expressed in their continuous poverty or criminality, were traits that were probably passed on through successive generations and were visible through such outward signs as the texture of the skin and the shape of the jaw. Well-known national and regional characteristics, such as eye and hair colour, body shape, muscular strength and so on, could also be accounted for through physiognomic inheritance. In short, every visible aspect of the individual's appearance was physiognomical and thus spoke of the submerged universe of personality, character, emotionality and temperament.

Lavater's systematic analysis of character assumed a male norm. He had the male image in mind as he discoursed on the meaning of the forehead, its wrinkles, the colour of the eyes and the shape of the chin. The differences between men and women were for Lavater oppositional, not unlike many of our contemporary depictions of the sexes. Women were 'more pure, tender, delicate, irritable, affectionate, flexible and patient' than men; they were made of a 'primary matter' that was more 'elastic than that of man'. Further, 'the female thinks not profoundly; profound thought is the power of the man.' As if to state proleptically our contemporary stereotypes, Lavater declared that 'women feel more'; they are flexible and bending where men are firm, straight and steadfast. Men were 'serious', women were 'gay'; men were 'rough and hard', 'brown' and 'angular', women were 'smooth and soft', 'fair' and 'round'; and when these expectations were violated women 'are no longer women, but abortions' (Lavater 1885:400–3).

In Lavater's views on women there is less assurance; for instance, he regarded the physically plain woman as making an excellent housewife; however, such a woman needed to be treated calmly, with a position of detachment because she was potentially volatile. 'Women with brown, hairy or bristly warts on the chin, especially the underpart of the chin, or the neck, are commonly industrious, active, good housewives', but 'they talk much' and so 'must be treated with circumspect, calm friendship, and kept at a distance by a mildly-cold dignity of demeanour' (Lavater 1885:481, rule seventy-three). Despite such references to women, overall, Lavater had little to say about them because he assumed that the main force and the norm of a society was the male.

Lavater had detractors who argued that the system of physiognomy was fallible. The most common of its weaknesses was thought to be the detection of subtefuge. It could happen that people misjudged one another or were fooled by appearances of beauty and virtue. Lavater acknowledged that it may be possible to imitate certain appearances under some circumstances but, his confident response was that long-term dissimulation was impossible. Certain parts of the body could not lie, for example, the shape of the head, eye colour, thickness or thinness of the lips and one's general skeletal frame or boniness; these could not be disguised. Furthermore, when the individual attempted to feign a particular appearance, Lavater maintained that it would be unsuccessful. For instance, shaping one's appearance to effect the signs of goodness and virtue would not result in the individual's acquiring these valued attributes. The links between moral character and physical appearance were strong and true and they could not be acquired simply from the vanity of imitation. Lavater did not advance a physiognomic view that admitted to the absorption of experiences that would alter both appearance and character. So, to act and look as if one were a particular character would not result in those character traits being absorbed into one's appearance, even if one should maintain such an act over a lengthy period of time. Indeed, this view protected Lavater from the criticism that appearances could be deceptive. Although, misjudgements and misrepresentations may occur, Lavater was confident that dissimulation could not be effected for any length of time; eventually, the true character of the individual would always be visible to the trained eye of the beholder (1885:45–9, 84).

Lavater's system of character analysis had one hundred physiognomical rules (1885:461–91). Those parts of the body with the most rules, and which were deemed the most accurately reflective of character were the forehead (rules seven to fourteen), the wrinkles on the forehead (rules fifteen to twenty), the eyes (rules twenty-one to thirty-three), nose (rules thirty-seven to forty-four) and the mouth (rules forty-seven to fifty-six). Although Lavater confessed to knowing little about women he produced six rules about them (rules seventy-one to seventy-six). His reasoning was that if others with less knowledge of physiognomy took on the task of analysing women, they would damage the credibility of physiognomy overall; so he felt obliged to produce some rules about women in order to protect his physiognomic schema from potential misrepresentation. Lavater maintained that the practice of physiognomy was like that of philosophy, 'a little philosophy leads to Atheism, much to Christianity' (1885:397). By the same token, if a dilettante applied physiognomy to women, a diluted analysis would appear which could undermine the integrity of the entire system.

A bedrock belief of the physiognomic perspective was the association of similarity. Lavater strenuously advised, as did others after him, that an individual should not enter close relations with another who was physically dissimilar. In rule ninety-five, Lavater stated that 'if thou hast a long high forehead, contract no friendship with an almost spherical head; if thou has an almost spherical head, contract no friendship with a long high bony forehead – such dissimilarity is especially unsuitable to matrimonial union' (Lavater 1885:487). Echoing the sentiment was the nineteenth-century resident of Scarborough and 'practical phrenologist' Professor Blackburne, who stated in his book, *Love, Courtship and Marriage (Phrenologically Considered) With Useful Hints How To Make a Wise Choice, and Thus Live Happily through Life*, 'in order to secure true reciprocity of feeling and union of soul, and thus obtain the largest amount of happiness in the married state, select a companion whose phrenological development and temperament for the most part resemble your own – avoiding extremes' (1881:9). Lavater's other warnings about friends and marriage partners were specifically stated in rules eighty-three and ninety through to ninety-three; they advised to 'avoid great eyes in small countenances, with small noses, in persons of little size'; avoid as well, 'large, bulky persons with small eyes; round, full hanging cheeks, puffed lips, and a chin resembling a purse or bag'; also avoid the man 'who walks slowly, bending forwards', and 'be circumspect as possible in the presence of a corpulent choleric man, who continually speaks loud' (Lavater 1885:485–7).

The major part of Lavater's work was the provision of exact descriptions of those specific body and facial parts which precisely revealed the individual's character. For example, the forehead was an eloquent feature which boldly declared the general dimensions of the individual's character; 'the more curved and cornerless the outline, the more tender and flexible the character'. With square foreheads, 'with extensive temples and firm eyebones ... circumspection and certainty of character' was shown (Lavater 1885:380–2). With 'foreheads inclining to be long, with close-drawn wrinkleless skin, which exhibit no lively cheerful wrinkles even in their few moments of joy', they foretold of a person who was 'cold, malign, suspicious, severe, selfish, censorious, conceited', who was mean and seldom forgave (Lavater 1885, rule nine). A forehead without arches, hollows or indentations indicated a common, mediocre character who was 'destitute of ideas' (rule twelve). However, the display of parallel, regular wrinkles which were not too deep suggested that the person was 'very intelligent, wise, rational and justly thinking' (rule sixteen), and when the wrinkles on the forehead were too deep, they indicated a weakness of mind, stupidity, avarice and a character that lacked sensibility (rule eighteen). The subtlety of the physiognomic system was well illustrated with the interpretation it gave of facial wrinkles. This example also illustrates how astute was Lavater at self-promotion: he stated that in order to distinguish the parallel, oblique wrinkles, which indicated a poor suspicious mind, from the parallel wrinkles, which indicated a wise rational sensibility, and to distinguish them yet further from the deep wrinkles which suggested an avaricious and stupid character, much devotion to the study of his rules and recommendations was required (rules fifteen, sixteen, eighteen).

An equally important feature of the face in Lavater's system of analysis was the nose. He regarded 'the nose to be the foundation, or abutment, of the brain ... A beautiful nose will never be found accompanying an ugly countenance. An ugly person may have fine eyes, but not a handsome nose' (1885:390). More precisely, downturned noses indicated a character of heartlessness, coldness and ill-humour in an individual who was prone to melancholy, while upturned noses indicated a character inclined to pleasure and ease in individuals who also had the unpleasant features of pertinacity and jealousy (Lavater 1885, rules thirty-eight and thirty-nine). The colour of the eyes, too, was an important index of character. Lavater claimed that 'blue eyes are, generally, more significant of weakness, effeminancy and yielding, than brown and black', while 'grey eyes, generally, denote deceit, instability and indecision', and large eyes, when they were prominent, indicated a covetous greedy temperament (1885:383, 388). The mouth, lips and chin were also telling features. Indeed, 'whatever is in the mind is communicated to the mouth', thus, making the lips into instantaneous summaries of character: 'firm lips, firm character; weak lips, and quick in motion, weak and wavering character' (1885:392, 394). The chin was a measure of moral strength, 'the pointed chin is generally held to be a sign of acuteness and craft ... the soft, fat double chin, generally points out the epicure' (1885:396).

Physiognomy was a means of calculating and understanding the invisible from the visible; it assumed that the nature of human actions and intentions were recorded in the obvious signs of the face and body. The physiognomic interpretations of the face and body are worth exploring in greater detail because some of the associations posited between certain character traits and physical features will be recognized as contemporary and familiar. Indeed, the interpretations of character made by the physiognomists may not always seem remote and quaint at all, but may, instead, have modern resonances for us.

In our present-day recognition and sense of familiarity with many of the ideas of the physiognomists, we arrive at the suggestion that certain human preoccupations with reading character and working out the rules of interpersonal commerce, are of an enduring nature. Furthermore, our unattributed and largely unrecognized familiarity with physiognomic interpretations of character suggests that these ideas have had a remarkable longevity. After all, if we are unwittingly using an ancient form of character analysis such as physiognomy in a modern world where the plasticity of appearance (made possible through the use of cosmetics, surgical treatments, bioengineering and so on) has been taken for granted, then we are implicitly endorsing the perspicacity of these old perspectives. Lavater may have warned that we cannot get away with deception for any length of time but, in the late twentieth century, with diet, drugs and surgical interventions available to us, we can be more confident of perpetrating deceptions in our physical appearances which will endure for decades. Even though Lavater did not anticipate the modern surgical techniques which can alter skeletal and muscular characteristics, the strong interest we have in changing body shape emphasizes the importance we place on appearance and this bolsters Lavater's assertion that we are all 'instinctive physiognomists'.

After the detailed and systematic enunciation of the physiognomic system by Lavater, others such as Wells (1867), Cruse (1874) and Spon (1934) added their embellishments. That they saw a need to add to the body of Lavater's work can be interpreted as further evidence of the enduring popularity of the physiognomic vision. The treatise by Samuel Wells, *New Physiognomy, or, Signs of Character, as manifested through Temperament and External Forms, and especially in the Human Face Divine* was published in 1867, almost a century after

29

Lavater's principal work of 1775–8. On the title-page of Wells's work, Shakespeare has been carefully quoted, 'I do believe thee! I saw his heart in his face' – which, presumably, was a poetic summation of the physiognomic position. Wells drew heavily on Lavater and accepted that 'form indicates character' (Wells 1867:19). He defined physiognomy in much the same way as Lavater, as 'a knowledge of the relation between the external and the internal, and of the signs through which the character of the mind is indicated by the developments of the body' (1867:13). He contended that 'inward goodness' corresponded immediately and directly to 'outward beauty' (1867:25). That is, a correspondence existed 'between the physical system and the spiritual principle which animates and controls it – between the manifest effect and the hidden cause'. The proof of that correspondence was in the individual's face, 'because it is there that the greater number of the signs of character are most clearly and legibly inscribed' (1867:81).

For Wells, more than for Lavater, other body parts were important in revealing character. Physiognomy 'takes into account the temperament; the shape of the body; the size and form of the head; the texture of the skin; the quality of the hair, the degree of functional activity, and other physiological conditions as well as the features of the face' (Wells 1867:80–1). Where Lavater had been sceptical of arguing that experiences altered physiognomy, Wells added this idea to the theory. He considered that the analytic power of physiognomy was capable of revealing character from facial and body features even after circumstances and experiences had impinged themselves upon the individual.

> As we look, so we feel, so we act, and so we are. But we may *direct* and *control* even our *thoughts*, our *feelings*, and our *acts*, and thus, to some extent – by the aid of grace – become what we will. We can be temperate or intemperate; virtuous or vicious; hopeful or desponding; generous or selfish; believing or skeptical; prayerful or profane, and our bodies, our brains, and our features readily adapt themselves and clearly indicate the lives we lead and the characters we form. (Wells 1867:3)

1 Character as Immanent in Appearance

According to Wells, while human character was expressed in external form, some recognition must also be given to the shaping of one's external form by one's own will. Wells maintained that the face could be improved by a religious life or, conversely, spoiled by the indulgence of immodest passions, say, for alcohol or tobacco. Thus, Wells's physiognomic reading of human appearance gave both a prediction of the individual's desires and a summary of his/her actions and accomplishments to date. It allowed for experiences to be transposed into external features, thereby, providing friends and associates with the opportunity to read one's history from one's appearance.

Wells, like Lavater and others, regarded physiognomic analysis as a rule of social life; 'we instinctively, as it were, judge the qualities of things by their outward forms' (1867:17). He, like Lavater, encountered the criticism that physiognomists could not always detect dissimulation in the individual. Indeed, once the principal physiognomic rule was understood that character was immanent in appearance, which also meant that we were judged by others by our appearance, then we would recognize countless situations in which it would be expedient for us to employ deceptions and disguises. Wells dismissed the complaint with the comment, '"appearances" are said to be "often deceitful". They are seemingly so; but in most cases, if not in all, it is our observation that is in fault. We have but to look again, and more closely and carefully, to pierce the disguise, when the thing will *appear to be* just what it *is*. Appearances do not often deceive the intelligent observer' (1867:17 original emphasis).

Where deceptions in appearance were perpetrated, Wells could still mount an argument which claimed these as proof of his system. He reasoned that the veracity of physiognomy was even more firmly established by seeing how readily its ideas were exploited by those wishing to deceive. Thus, 'if a knave try to appear like an honest man, it is because he recognises the fact that honesty has a certain characteristic expression, and knows that his fellow-men are aware what this expression is' (Wells 1867:17). For Wells, instances of dissimulation were excellent grounds for proselytizing physiognomy because these deliberate attempts to deceive could not be successful if, as he claimed, one knew physiognomy well enough to read character fully and subtly.

A further reason for the study of physiognomy, according to Wells, was that it enabled individuals to be improved. By being able to read character and, thereby, judge strengths, weaknesses, virtues and faults, we could be prepared to take actions to 'reconstruct ourselves on an improved plan, correcting unhandsome deviations, moderating excessive developments, supplying deficiencies, molding our characters' (Wells 1867:22). As human happiness depended upon interactions with others and what others thought of us, both of which were largely determined by appearance, Wells could maintain that a facility with physiognomic principles was essential. It was a matter of logic that our happiness could be increased if we knew, from a study of physiognomy, what others thought of us and what we should know of others. Physiognomy was the key to proper sociation and, in turn, increased human happiness. Furthermore, it was the means for improving society because it promised to bring about more harmonious exchanges between the body and brain, which, in turn, would produce a general elevation of the human spirit (Wells 1867:4). Wells acknowledged that physiognomy was 'not yet entitled to the dignity of a science' (1867:17), but he believed it to have the necessary elements of a science. He maintained physiognomy was still in its scientific infancy, conveniently overlooking the history of the idea which stretched back to antiquity.

Wells's exposition of the theory remained close to the work of Lavater in that he used Lavater's general and specific rules as signs of human character. Wells stated, as had Lavater, that certain wrinkles on the forehead indicated the 'cold, malign, suspicious, severe, selfish, censorious, conceited, mean' nature of the individual (Wells 1867:30; Lavater 1885:464), and a smoother surface on the forehead indicated that the person was 'common, mediocre, destitute of ideas, and incapable of invention' (Wells 1867:31; Lavater 1885, rule twelve). The correspondences between the two theorists continued with the rules on interpreting the eyes and mouth. When the eyes were blue and large, the individual could be thought of as having a ready and great capacity; individuals with small black eyes were of a cunning disposition; others with eyes hooded under heavy lids were intellectually brilliant; those individuals with weak, small eyebrows containing little hair were of a feeble constitution with a melancholic weakness of mind. With Wells, as with Lavater, the nose was capable of revealing much of human character because it was a summation of the forehead as well as the root or anchorage of the under part of the face. According to Wells, upturned, retroussé noses indicated a personality inclined to pleasure and capable of jealousy. A downturned nose suggested the individual was heartless, incommunicative, malicious, sarcastic, melancholic and hypochondriacal. Where the cheeks were fully curved, the individual suffered from stupidity, where the chin was long, broad and thick, the individual was rude, harsh, proud and violent with people.

Wells regarded the mouth as a sign of the individual's observable capacities, while the forehead signified the individual's potential. When these were in contradiction, when the mouth suggested one view and the forehead another, then the observer should be well-warned, such an individual was not to be trusted. A small mouth accompanied by a small nose and arched forehead revealed the individual as fearful, vain and ineloquent. A well-proportioned mouth, but with large lips, suggested that the individual was gross, lascivious and indelicate, and a mouth that was out of proportion relative to the size of the eyes, reflected a character prone to folly and wickedness (Wells 1867:30–50). Wells also made use of humoural theory with its classical quartet of personalities. He described an individual with a low hairline and narrow forehead as having a fiery, choleric character; an individual with short fingernails as energetic, efficient, enthusiastic and a sanguine personality; the individual with cold dry skin and large earlobes as pensive, intellectual and of melancholic character; and those with broad, thick feet and hands, who were lazy but, nonetheless, graceful in movement, as phlegmatic in character (1867:55).

An enduring claim of the physiognomists was that the face revealed the moral character of the individual, either in repose

33

or when the play of muscles under the skin gave movement to the face. (An alternative view, that of the pathognomics, focused exclusively on the changes to appearance brought about by the play of the passions over the face.) As physiognomy became increasingly popular during the nineteenth century, and more imitations and derivations of it appeared, the techniques and signs used to reveal the self became even more formulaic and exact. Thus, Cruse, in his treatise, *Phrenology Made Easy* (1874), could precisely identify forty unique characteristics of personality from forty precisely specifiable physical formations of the face. Cruse defined phrenology and physiognomy as 'the Art of Discovering the Character of the Mind, as expressed in the lines and features of the Human Countenance'. He, like Wells, accepted that experiences could fashion appearances; thus, he regarded any idiosyncracies of the individual as important, and so maintained that 'due attention should be observed of any Change of feature through accident or ill health. It is also necessary to consider the influence of Education, in forming the dispositions of Individuals' (1874:1– 2).

Cruse's physiognomy was remarkably precise in so far as he correlated single emotions with exact details of the face. For example, he could read individual levels of self-esteem from the stiffness of the upper lip, a sense of independence from the length of the throat and the individual's generosity from the closeness of the lips at the corners. Further, violent passions were signified by a broad chin with an uneven surface, pride or scorn from the curl of the upper lip, congeniality from the prominence of the chin, purity from the closeness of the lips to each other, selfishness from smooth lips, constant love from the breadth of the upper part of the cheek, suspicion from the point of the nose downwards, reason from the length of the wing of the nostril as it pointed upwards, and impulsiveness from the fullness of the cheeks at the side of the mouth.

Cruse claimed to tell, from a visual calculation of the thickness of the lower part of the nose, whether an individual had the ability to draw comparisons or to reason through the use of similes. As well, he maintained that the individual's level of enquiry was reflected in the upward turn of the point of the nose, and his or her propensity to aggression was seen in the prominence of the nose's upper portions. Characteristics of secretiveness were revealed by the breadth across the nostrils, and the individual's inclination to ostentation was shown in the fullness of the outward turn of the upper lip.

The increasing precision of physiognomy to identify characteristics of mind and sensibility from the physical features of the face continued into the twentieth century with the work of Spon, who declared physiognomy to be 'a method by which the character or properties of animate and inanimate objects are disclosed by an examination of their shape, colour, or outward appearance' (1934:1). Like others before him, Spon was convinced that 'everybody practises physiognomy daily throughout their lives either consciously or unconsciously, and nobody doubtless will deny the importance of knowing what behaviour to expect from the people with whom we must associate both in public or private intercourse' (1934:2).

Spon's physiognomy was remarkably exact. He declared the nose to be 'the index of the whole collective mind' (1934:10). The size of the nose reflected power whereas its shape indicated whether one was artistic, literary, poetic, critical, philosophic, dramatic, athletic, argumentative and so on. A tipped or retroussé nose reflected a hollow character with a fondness for change and novelty; it also indicated brightness and wit (1934:18). A more bony rather than muscular nose, which stood well above the planes of the face, indicated an argumentative character. Spon also identified a 'commercial nose' which showed powers of acquisitiveness, that is, it was well proportioned and bulky, and indicative of the owner's capacity to withstand 'the anxiety and suspense that speculation involves' (1934:31). There were also melancholic noses, which pointed downward, dishonest noses with nostrils too thin, revengeful noses which were high and bony and noses which were abnormal because they were too long or too short (1934:33–5).

The eyes were important in Spon's physiognomy and he was characteristically exact about what they revealed. Black eyes reflected a violent disposition and an intensity of passion; brown eyes suggested an amiable character; blue eyes indicated

35

a coolness of feeling; grey eyes revealed intellectuality, and green eyes were indicative of a cruel, sly and suspicious character. Spon regarded the brightness and fineness of the eyes as reflecting qualities in the brain and the nervous system. A dull eye indicated a coarse, common mind and a round eye, with its greater movement, indicated finer qualities such as mental agility and intelligence. A bulging eye suggested a shallow mind, receding eyes revealed an organic weakness in the individual which, in turn, produced a timidity of mind, and small eyes foretold of the individual's feeble mental powers, secretiveness and inability to represent ideas and intentions clearly (Spon 1934:43–51). Like the nose, the eyes could express 'primary' characteristics such as whether individuals were artistic, reflective, agreeable, linguistic, political, untruthful, cruel, observing, licentious, shallow, gluttonous and secretive. Eyes that were shaped downward were common to individuals involved with politics in that they indicated a propensity for misrepresentation. Such eyes could also be found in individuals who were untruthful. Spon defined abnormal eyes as too round and too wide. Women had 'monogamic' eyes which were well opened with rounded corners and true curves along the lid. Men had 'polygamic' eyes which were long narrow openings with sharp angles at the corners (1934:55–69).

Spon, like Cruse and Wells, entertained the idea that the individual's idiosyncratic experiences could be translated into revealing features of appearance. This view of physiognomy has a contemporary relevance because it accepted the idea that appearances could be fashioned and that individuals could shape a particular visage for themselves, yet, still retain a belief that character was immanent in appearance. Such a view may seem contradictory; on the one hand, it argued that character was immanent in appearance and was an integral part of the individual's existence, yet, on the other hand, identity was capable of being fashioned from the individual's deliberate and self-produced choices to look and act in a particular way. However, the contradiction was treated as contrived. The facts of the matter were taken to be that physical appearance and social conduct were two sides of the same coin.

Spon absorbed the dual aspects of the fashioned and given self into his physiognomic system when he determined that facial wrinkles were both reflections of specific experiences and signs of a developed intellect. Spon regarded the wrinkles and folds around the eyes as incisive tools for character analysis. He interpreted the muscular activity of the face as an expression of intellectual activity; thus the resulting wrinkles were to be seen as records of the individual's mental activity, emotions, thoughts and passions. Indeed, so important were the wrinkles and folds of the face that Spon considered they should be viewed as summary signs of the self. He warned that 'the reader should not deceive himself by thinking that he or she can erase or modify these wrinkles at will. They are indelible records of people's past life and indicate their customary actions, choice of speech and degree of thought' (1934:53).

As facial wrinkles were regarded as highly expressive, too many wrinkles over the face indicated a life passed in petty cares; wrinkles under the eyes, especially in the young, indicated dissipation; straight parallel wrinkles across the forehead indicated clarity of thought, while other wrinkles on the forehead indicated doggedness, concentration and perserverance. The heavy wrinkle across the bridge of the nose reflected an ability to command others (Spon 1934:195), and it could also indicate a chronic condition of muscular fatigue (1934:9). Spon's final assessment of facial wrinkles was to acclaim their value as indicators of character; to his mind, 'a smooth shining face without any wrinkles belongs to a suave, plausible, flattering, dishonest and unprincipled character and one who's all things to all people' (1934:198).

Spon's attention to facial minutiae was pronounced, even the eyelashes being considered highly indicative of character. Long, curved eyelashes suggested muscularity, short lashes indicated rudeness and directness, while long, silky, fine lashes reflected a refinement of sentiments (Spon 1934:77–9). The eyebrows, too, showed character: when they were spaced far apart, they indicated an absence of practical good sense; when continuous across the bridge of the nose they showed conceit. Eyebrows could show the mathematical, scientific, artistic, imaginative, deceptive, inventive and practical nature of the individual. When curved they showed shrewdness, when straight and bar-like they showed intelligence (1934:83).

Spon assumed an immediate correspondence between the appearance of the body and the individual's character traits. Thus, a mouth that was crooked or disproportionate indicated a corresponding skew in character: a crooked mouth showed criminality, and disproportionate lips meant viciousness. The mouth also reflected the individual's artistic, conversational, oratorial and meditative capacities. Those who discoursed on serious subjects had a short upper lip. In contrast, a protruding lower lip suggested stupidity (Spon 1934:93–113). A dimpled chin indicated a sensuous nature, a receding chin meant weakness of character, a fat or double chin was indicative of dishonesty, while a flabby chin was associated with a feeble intellect (1934:141). Dimples in the cheeks proved good health in an individual who was also characteristically good-natured and readily showed affection and an amorous disposition (1934:152–6).

Hair colour and the texture of skin were other features identified by Spon as revealing of character. He viewed curly hair as indicative of a quick temper and a changeable, vivacious nature; gold or blonde hair revealed an exalted mind; red hair proclaimed the intensity and quick temper of its owner; straight hair indicated a direct and morally courageous nature; thin hair suggested physical delicacy but a keen perception, even brilliance, although the individual was also troubled with shyness and irritability (Spon 1934:190–5). Spon further characterized fat, big-boned individuals as lazy, athletic individuals as prone to jealousy, individuals with short stature as suspicious of others, and those with dark skin as being selfish and revengeful (1934:283). The prognathic individual had an undeveloped intellect and a primitive morality (1934:168); the courageous individual had large ears which stood out from the head, while broad, flexible ears reflected commercial acumen, and well-hollowed-out ears were associated with a musical nature (1934:176–80).

Spon's detailed physiognomic system of character analysis granted a close fit between the visible aspects of the individual's appearance and the intangible features of personal identity. In this assumed correspondence, the physiognomists of the nineteenth and twentieth centuries were not alone. Another example of a close correspondence between human physiology and character could be found in Lombroso's theory of criminality. Cesare Lombroso's 1876 treatise on human criminality provided copious details of the physiognomy of deviants, and claimed an ability to predict the criminal potential of the individual from his or her morphology. According to Lombroso, once identified as potentially criminal, individuals should be put under surveillance and, at the first signs of their criminal nature, they should be exiled from society. The development of a systematic taxonomy of physical stigmata, that was both quantitative and comprehensive, had immense appeal to those nineteenth-century authorities who were concerned with social order and the containment of oppositional ideas and conduct. Foucault (1977; 1980), in his histories of the regulatory social institutions of the prison and the hospital, has emphasized the value of surveillance and how the scientific categorization of the body has provided the modern technique par excellence for imposing a repressive social order.

The same concerns, less explicitly acknowledged, appealed to the criminologist Cesare Lombroso, who conceived of his physiognomic system as a fitting tool by which to forge a better social order. As a liberal and reformist thinker, Lombroso's identification of criminals from physical appearances, before they were a menace to others, was made in an effort to minimize the impact of any disintegrative elements which could threaten the social order. Lombroso's descriptions of criminals employed many of the tenets of physiognomy. He described the criminal as commonly having a small cranial capacity, heavy and developed jaws, abnormal and asymmetrial cranium, large outstanding ears and a crooked or flat nose. Often criminals were colour-blind, they had precocious wrinkles and a low forehead, they were often left-handed, had curly abundant hair, thick lips, small eyes and large noses (see also Weschler 1982; Lewontin et al. 1984:53). In addition, criminals were insensitive to pain as demonstrated by their proclivity for tattoos. Their skulls were unusually thick, they had long arms and

I The Physiognomic Body

prehensile feet with a mobile big toe (see also Gould 1980:222–8).

Another subdivision of physiognomy was phrenology, an intellectual enterprise which has had a more illustrious career than its progenitor. The phrenologists emerged in the early decades of the nineteenth century and immediately claimed the status of a science. In Edinburgh a protracted battle over the definition of science was carried out using the example of phrenology, during which the status of phrenology was differentiated from that of physiognomy. The principal tenet of phrenology rested upon the character of the brain, which was assumed to be the organ of the mind. This was an interest which the physiognomists never shared. To the phrenologists, the mind was the sum total of thirty-five distinct and innate functions which were each specifically located in the brain. It followed that the size of the brain or cerebral organ was an indication of the power of each of these functions. Thus, the size and shape of the brain could be taken as a sign of the individual's capacity for certain experiences and activities. The phrenologist studied the contours of the head on the assumption that the human skull followed the shape of the brain, and by tracing the exterior of the head an analysis could be made of the individual's talents and character. Not only this, but an individual's mental functions and by implication the nature of his or her character and soul were represented by the bumps and grooves that the brain impressed upon the skull (see Shapin 1975; 1979; Gould 1984).

From these early audacious claims, the study of phrenology followed a more rigorous path and came to constitute an impetus for the more exact localization of physical functions in the brain such as those identified in Broca's and Wernicke's areas. The localizations have subsequently contributed greatly to modern neurophysiology. In contrast, the scientization of physiognomy has not been as successful. Physiognomy cannot be attributed with the founding of a modern, reputable science of character analysis but, even so, its ratiocination has endured and can be seen to affect contemporary theories of human character. Gould (1980), for example, has documented how physical characteristics such as race and sex have been used, in

40

modern times, as the basis for measuring human intelligence. He has suggested that these exercises in physiognomic reasoning are mismeasures of human characteristics and it is remarkable that they continue to appear in the late twentieth century.

The physiognomic perspective has descended from ancient roots into the twentieth century with its fundamental tenet intact – that character is immanent in appearance. In his analysis of nineteenth- and twentieth-century literature, Tytler (1982) has argued that our literary heritage resonates with biologically founded explanations of human conduct and there is surprisingly little critical interrogation of that intellectual heritage. For example, the late nineteenth-century novelist, George Gissing (1857–1903), who was celebrated for his advanced and enlightened social attitudes, nonetheless, subscribed to the physiognomic perspective in his work. In *The Odd Women*, he has described the character of his protagonist through her physical features.

> She sat down with him as a male acquaintance might have done ... He delighted in the frankness of her speech; it was doubtful whether she regarded any subject as improper for discussion ... Part cause of this, perhaps, was her calm consciousness that she had not a beautiful face ... Studying her features, he saw how fine was their expression. The prominent forehead, with its little unevenness that meant brains; the straight eyebrows, strongly marked, with deep vertical furrows generally drawn between them ... the high-bridged nose, thin and delicate; the intellectual lips, a protrusion of the lower one, though very slight ... Probably, her constitution was very sound; she had good teeth, and a healthy brownish complexion. (1977:101–2)

If progressive forms of nineteenth-century literature such as that of Gissing employed physiognomic reasoning, it can be safely assumed, Tytler says, that physiognomic assumptions were widely accepted as natural laws of everyday practices. Such a conclusion would be consonant with Lavater's suggestion that we are all physiognomists, even without knowing it, because we commonly interpret so much of the other's character from appearance. Another comment on the banality of these ideas is provided by the contemporary British novelist

and critic, A. S. Byatt. Byatt has recognized that an explanation
of human conduct based upon a reading of physical features
is a practice deeply embedded within the common stock of
knowledge; she has, however, acknowledged the intellectual
truancy of the idea and the detrimental effect it has upon our
social relations.

> It is amazing, when we stop to contemplate the variety, the de-
> vious differences, the secret predilections and emotional histories
> behind or under individual faces, that a culture should so stead-
> fastly ascribe one physiognomy to one habit of mind, or morals.
> But we have done, and do, and this must affect the innocent lords
> and owners of archetypal faces. (1986:208)

The antiquated theories of physiognomists, phrenologists
and astrologers have survived the centuries to continue to claim
that external physical appearances correspond with internal
psychological and moral predispositions. Physiognomy has
also been used to uncover human intentions, inner feelings,
virtues, vices and the workings of the imagination. In the
twentieth century, Paolo Mantegazza, for example, has reworked much of Lavater in order to establish the study of
clothing and bodily adornment as an important part of the
physiognomic enterprise. His concern has been to show that
the continuous existence of fashions in garments can also be
used, physiognomically, to explicate the inner human character. Mantegazza has reasoned that fashion makes little sense
unless it is the case that people use it as a reliable means of
judging character as well as a method for making certain character traits visible to others. It was Mantegazza's contention
that human emotions pass 'voluntarily or involuntarily' into
the textures of clothes as they are worn. Thus, 'dress is certainly one of the human elements by which races, nations, and
individuals express most of themselves' (n.d.:298). He has
further maintained that the more clothing we possess the more
opportunities there are for our emotions to express themselves
and, conversely, the less clothed we are, or the less fashionable
we are, the less we have to express. In this way, Mantegazza's
theory unintentionally complements the modern consumer

ethic of the industrialized societies which has incrementally transformed the human body into a repository for the myriad commodities we are urged to buy in order to demonstrate to others our inner, less visible, qualities of character.

The longevity of the physiognomic perspective and the multitude of interpretations and applications it has generated lend the perspective an aura of impressive forcefulness. It seems as if questions of its validity have been subsumed by its longevity. For centuries the idea that human character has a physiognomic and biological base has been, in one form or another, part of the common stock of social knowledge. In contemporary society, there are examples of the belief in modern literature, mass advertising, popular psychology, and social commentary. For instance, Sontag (1980) has recently described Walter Benjamin as a saturnine personality; she begins her analysis of his intellectual contribution with a physical description that uses the terms of the ancient physiognomists and astrologers. The saturnine personality was 'apathetic, indecisive, slow' (1980:114); such a personality was also blundering, stubborn and myopic, whilst simultaneously being highly perceptive. Sontag's description of Benjamin using terms concerned with his physical attributes, 'a slack, corpulent figure', 'myopic', 'blocky, huge', 'pudgy', 'opaque' and so on (1980:109–10), make these physical features into evocations of character which, in his case, indicate a brooding, complex intelligence.

The evolutionary biologist, Stephen Jay Gould, has suggested that we have placed too much importance upon biological explanations of certain cultural forms; in particular, he has in mind the high social value we have granted to human physical appearance. Gould has discussed the theory of neoteny to illustrate the point. Neoteny refers to a biological argument which states that human evolution has been significantly influenced by the retention of juvenile physical features. The word literally means 'holding youth' (Gould 1980:63) and the theory, derived from Louis Bolk's (1929) 'foetalization theory', claims that humans have evolved through progressive juvenilization. While other primates and mammals have a stage of juvenility in the course of their maturation, it is significantly humans alone who retain their juvenile features

43

into adulthood. The outstanding characteristics of juvenility include a bulging forehead, small jaws, large eyes and an overall larger head size in relation to the size of the human body (Serpell 1986:62). The claims of neoteny are that we are better off, that is, our chances of survival are increased because of our juvenile features. Gould (1980:219) has further quoted Havelock Ellis (1894) as saying 'the progress of the race has been a progress in youthfulness.' Ashley Montagu's (1974) argument of the natural superiority of women, first advanced in the late 1940s, is another example of neotenic thinking.

The theory of neoteny suggests that the value accorded to a youthful appearance, the cultural premium placed upon physical appearance and the search for eternal youth and beauty in such pursuits as fashionability and cosmetic surgery have their origins in the associative attributes of youth. For instance, if we retain a juvenile appearance, if we stay looking younger longer, it may seem as if we also possess other life-enhancing characteristics of the neotenic, namely, that we are still maturing and are engaged in intensive learning. In the animal world, this has meant a greater chance of biological survival and success. To carry the idea through to human society, it may seem that the longer we look younger the more likely we are to be socially successful.

Gould (1983:81–91) has analysed the progressive rejuvenation of Walt Disney's cartoon character, Mickey Mouse, to support the idea that unexplicated neotenic beliefs may be an integral feature of modern social life. However, his purpose in the analysis has not been to prove the importance of biological forces on our styles of social conduct but, the reverse, to illustrate how readily we endorse biologically based explanations of social conduct when there is little evidence to support such an application. In this article on Mickey Mouse and elsewhere (Gould 1980), Gould has asked, what is the effect of appropriating biological ideas into the social sphere: 'why are we so intrigued by hypotheses of innate disposition?' and why do we commonly attribute acts of aggression, violence and greed to genetic endowments, when we also like to claim the opposite, that the hallmark of human progress has been our ability to overcome the biological determinations of inheritance

1 Character as Immanent in Appearance

and nature (Gould 1980:228)? The cultural consequences of believing in biological theories of human behaviour are impossible to ascertain; however, their popularity as explanations of various forms of social conduct is unequivocal and that leads Gould to lament that we too readily invoke biological theories as explanations of more complex social conduct.

Gould's (1983:81–91) observations of the progressive rejuvenation of Mickey Mouse led to the conclusion that neotenic assumptions are accepted as axiomatic in much the same way as are physiognomic assumptions. In the early 1930s Mickey Mouse appeared thinner, sharper, physically more adult in appearance than he did in the late 1970s. Over the years, Mickey has become sequentially blander in appearance, 'progressively more juvenile' (Gould 1983:82). His new image has been conveyed by a rounding and enlarging of his physical features. Gould has measured the cartoon character's physical proportions over his life-span and found that Mickey's eyes have increased in size from 27 to 42 per cent of head length, his head has increased relative to his body from 42.7 to 48.1 per cent and the roundness of his head has increased substantially from a measure of 71.7 to 95.6 per cent (Gould 1983:82). These particular physical dimensions increased the appearance of juvenility; they made Mickey appear babyish, more vulnerable and clumsier. Gould has pointed out that these changes in appearance simultaneously paralleled changes in Mickey's temperament from an original mischievousness and ill-mannered, sometimes cruel posture, to a less offensive, more engaging and lovable personality. By the evolution of his appearance into a rounder, softer shape, Mickey has become more widely appealing because he seems more vulnerable and dependent on others.

A neotenic appearance supposedly enhances the survival rate of the individual because others are more willing to provide him or her with affection and support. The claims of neoteny are that the individual with more juvenile physical features will gain the support of others more readily and be more socially successful than those individuals with a less vulnerable appearance, such as those who are more angular (Alley 1980). Affection is supposedly elicted more readily where the object of

45

I The Physiognomic Body

affection, be it a human baby, chimpanzee or puppy, has distinctive juvenile features. Serpell (1986:67) has given an example of a mothering wolf being more responsive to Malamute pups than her own wolf pups because the Malamute pups were furrier, rounder, more dependent and clumsier than her own wolf pups. To Serpell this suggested that the neotenous appearance of the Malamute pups had elicited a more caring response from the mothering wolf, an idea which grants neoteny a stronger influence than maternity (see also Frank and Frank 1982).

Gould's (1983) analysis was intended to show that the changes to Mickey's appearance could not be thought of as unintended or accidental, nor could they be an unmediated expression of a subterranean rule of biology such as neoteny. He pointed out that changes to national symbols are not made without thorough forethought. Indeed, any changes to such prominent cultural and economic commodities such as Mickey Mouse, or, for that matter, Barbie dolls, Superman costumes or Coca-Cola, would entail extensive research of the consumer market (see Debord 1977; Haug 1986). It is more likely, then, that changes to Mickey Mouse were the result of a commercial strategy that indicated a more vulnerable appearance was consonant with and indicative of other contemporary values. Mickey's rejuvenation should not be read as a proof of the neotenic theory (Gould 1983:89) but as an illustration of an underlying, silent and largely unexplicated belief which resonates through modern society and places a high value on youthful appearance. Gould (1984) has argued elsewhere that we too commonly abuse biological theories by misemploying them as explanations of social behaviour.

Introducing the ideas of neoteny and physiognomy into this investigation of the modern self is not preliminary to a broader discussion of whether human beings are more in debt to biology or cultural circumstances for their habits of sociation. Indeed, the estimation of the validity of the neotenic and physiognomic arguments is well beyond the scope of this work. The value of the ideas, in this context, is restricted to their illustration of how identity is perceived and, in particular, the common propensity to invoke biological explanations for

46

essentially social processes. Physiognomy is an example of an authenticating narrative which employs biologically reductionist theories as explanations of observable patterns of social conduct. Both the physiognomic and neotenic arguments are of interest here as examples of the everyday emphasis given to individual physical appearance, and to the misapplication of biology to questions about human identity or character.

Reading personality from astrological birth signs,[1] or from obvious physical signs such as hair and eye colouring, physical fitness, rate of consumption and conspicuous displays of wealth, sensuality, fashionability and so on, is accepted as legitimate means for understanding the other. The language of the self and discourses on human character resonate with observations of physical attributes. The idea that abstract qualities of character can be seen in obvious signs of appearance continues to have a wide currency.

The disadvantage of accepting a biologically reductionist explanation of human character, such as physiognomy, is that it interferes with the quest to understand human character in relation to more abstract and difficult influences arising from social and historical conditions. The point of view of the present work is to show that our common conceptualizations of human character disadvantage us by granting to physical appearances a much greater value and power than is required for the successful sociation of individuals. By applying theories of inheritance and immanence to the problem of understanding human identity, be they physiognomic, neotenic or eidolonic (as shall be argued in the section on the fashioned self), we occlude the influence of the social, and we mischaracterize identity and moral posture as a private phenomenon, somehow resilient to much of the influence of the historical, philosophical and social.

In the next chapter, drawing on further representations of distinctive physical appearances as given in the literary and fictive universes of the Western tradition, we are again struck

---

[1] Astrological interpretations of character in the twentieth century are immensely popular. Most daily newspapers in the industrialized world publish a horoscope and people regularly read their 'stars'.

by the propensity to use the external and obvious elements of an individual's appearance and physical demeanour as the means of judging his or her character. Accepting the obvious world of appearance as a sign of the moral realm, commits us, as Eco has argued (1986), to a life lived at the surface where a reading of displays and exhibits is accepted as an appropriate limit to our thinking. Thus, if we read the signs and accept the appearance of the other as the key to his or her character, then we are at risk of avoiding the social encounter, with its inherent contestatory tension and its potential to provide more complex insights and understandings of the human condition. To accept the idea that character is immanent in appearance as an authenticating narrative is to avoid an encounter with the mysteries of the social; that we are prone to make this mistake is the argument of the present work.

2

Refining Appearance, Improving Character

Although the idea of being judged by one's physical appearance may seem a basic form of injustice, the use of appearance as an index to character is rampant. Not only is the idea found in naturalistic theories of human behaviour such as physiognomy and neoteny but it also operates in the figurative realms of literature and mythology, and in the applied areas of therapeutic medicine and related health fields. A wealth of psychological material produced in the past two decades strongly supports the adage that appearance counts. The data repeatedly confirm a body halo effect, that is, the more attractive the individual is considered to be, the more likely s/he will be attributed with other valued characteristics such as intelligence, wisdom, generosity and so on (Herman *et al.* 1986). The conclusion drawn from these studies is that being influenced by the appearance and physical features of an individual is a fundamental fact of sociation. From this conclusion, it seems as if physically distinctive individuals, irrespective of whether that distinctiveness is regarded as attractive or abhorrent, will be socially differentiated and, perhaps, exploited, ostracized and regarded with intolerance.

The argument presented in this chapter is that reading character from physical appearance is still common in contemporary society even though our awareness of how physical appearances can manipulate our sympathies and reactions, as evidenced by psychological data, is well enough known. Thus, the anomalous individual is still greeted with a degree of fear even though we know that physical anomalies and disfigurements are not mysterious events, nor are they visitations of the devil or evidence of the wrath of the gods or portents of future calamity. Indeed, current apprehension of the anomalous individual suggests that fears of the monstrous have not much diminished in the late twentieth century even though it is known that freakish life forms like Victor Frankenstein's monster cannot be manufactured in the home laboratory, that Siamese twins are not a sign of impending disaster but a statistical probability and that the distorted face and limbs of the hunchback of Notre Dame were probably the result of a rare inherited condition known as neurofibromatosis, like that suffered by the nineteenth-century 'elephant man', John Merrick.

In this modern era of medical and scientific hegemony, where the occurrence of human anomalies is often accompanied by rational explanations, still, the revulsion of the physically monstrous persists. It is not that an anomalous physical appearance conjures up a mysterious world of the supernatural, rather, such an appearance reminds us of the fragility of our social position. As Goffman has stated, 'the person who falls short' of 'certain moral, mental and physiognomic standards' is forced into a secondary status (1967:107). Without much difficulty, we can conjure up situations where this might happen to us.

Appearance matters a great deal and, as a result, the tools for affecting appearance, for altering physiognomy through surgery, exercise, cosmetics, clothing and so on, are sought after in our contemporary society and given a high social value. Even though we may be aware that appearance can be fashioned, its purported correspondence with the character of the individual persists. In our everyday commerce, much is still made of physical appearances as the summary of character.

The longevity of the idea that character can be deduced from appearances is explored, in this chapter, through early medical tracts and, then, in depictions of the human monstrous and anomalous in the literary canon. From a historical review of

50

the commonly stated causes of stigma and physical difference, it can be seen that explanations of the monstrous may have altered from supernatural to more materialistic causes but, significantly, fear of the monstrous seems undiminished. Medical practices in contemporary society show that a great deal of attention is paid to the modification of physical appearance in order to remediate features suggestive of the abnormal or monstrous. Willingness to refine appearance in accord with the prevailing definitions of the normal and attractive seems to support the idea that character is widely understood to be immanent in appearance.

Ours is a culture which values physical prowess and youthful beauty, and those who are maimed, deformed, diseased and aged often find themselves at some remove both physically and socially from the mainstream (see Goffman 1963). Indeed, to be physically disabled often commits the individual to a life of circumscribed social activity and secondary social value. Individuals who are physically different are seen to challenge the prevailing norms; they are the supernumeries and mysteries who strain the imagination about what is acceptable. Referring to defective infants, paediatricians Duff and Campbell (1979) have called them the 'socially dead', in recognition of their unlikely acceptance into mainstream society.

In most societies, bodily control, display and adornment have been translated into signs of social status and individual virtue. Régnier-Bohler (1988:360) has noted that since the Middle Ages, Western culture has represented the body, with increasing frequency, as an architectural metaphor of the society at large. In modern Western society, the individual's display of material competence and bodily control have been used to distinguish class and status and, in this way, a measure of personal qualities such as refinement and civility can be gauged from the carriage and control of the body (Veblen 1899; Lynes 1949; Fussell 1984). As the cultural anthropologist Mary Douglas (1973) has suggested, when the human body is regarded as emblematic of its social context, then it becomes a repository of a society's ideals of human conduct. Elias's (1978) history of manners has given rich details of the shifting expectations attached to bodily propriety. He has shown how social status has come to be read from the individual's posture, the manner in which s/he blows the nose, excretes bodily wastes and eats food. From his survey of four hundred years of interpersonal manners, Elias has noted how the minimalization of physical gestures and the increased sense of privacy attached to certain bodily functions have become gauges of social status. So it is now, when eating is managed without noise or the soiling of oneself, when physical exertion seems effortless and does not produce perspiration or noisy breathlessness, when laughter, anger and other strong emotions are modulated by minimal facial and bodily movements, we say that the individual is civilized, cultivated and attractive. In many ways, the performance of the body is a representation of the social order and, in our culture, it is specifically the control over and curtailment of bodily processes which reflect the highest level of social standing.

We enter the public domain as physical entities, and so it is by our body that we are initially judged by others and, in certain instances, stigmatized and set apart. Being stigmatized is dependent upon the system of social ranking at work. Sontag's studies (1977; 1989) of those with tuberculosis, cancer and AIDS give an insightful account of the continuously shifting cultural principles which underscore the ways in which human appearance is granted status and value. Sometimes it is the obese, or those with Alzheimer's disease, cerebral palsy or Down's syndrome, who are stigmatized. At other times, it is the schizophrenic, alcoholic and infertile who are set apart. Indeed, as Goffman (1963) has pointed out, it is possible to stigmatize any individual, given propitious circumstances.

The designation of stigma is not attached to a specific condition so much as being a social tool used for the regulation of the individual. The attachment of stigma to the individual allows for the imposition of an external order upon his or her life chances; for example, the presence of a stigma can function as a justification for the unequal distribution of social and economic resources, and the lesser valuation of specific individuals by the community at large. While stigma is most commonly a bestowed appellation some groups may embrace it, say, for political reasons, because they understand that stigma

52

is an exercise of power and a technique of social regulation. Stigma singles out the individual or social group; it is a tool in the construction of an exclusive culture, and it is the insignia by which an individual's social value and rank are publicly displayed. As stigma is the by-product of those rules which govern human exchange, the stigmatized features are, in most cases, the inversion of those cultivated practices which are the most highly valued.

Physically anomalous individuals have been longstanding objects for stigma. The physically different have been remarked upon throughout history with varying degrees of scorn, sympathy and interest. Some individuals have been made into freaks, that is, deliberately misshapen for ritual, aesthetic or commercial purposes. For example, Dworkin (1974) has suggested that the ancient Chinese habit of footbinding women was a deliberate act of mutilation disguised as a beauty treatment; the tight-lacing of Victorian women into boned corsets, which displaced the internal organs and frequently caused irreparable damage, was another deliberate means of shaping the physical appearance of women. The practice manufactured an anomalous body shape which, some have argued, increased a woman's status and opportunities for social freedom by making her more desirable and thereby better placed to negotiate her desires and needs (see Kunzle 1982). The same specious reasoning can be applied to the successful sideshow freak.

The physical freak has a history of making a livelihood from prurient exhibitionism and display. Before the age of the mass electronic media, fairs and circuses were a sanctuary for the physically different. St Bartholomew's Fair at Smithfield, commissioned by Henry I in 1133 and closed about 1849 was, for over six centuries, home to a variety of human curiosities, and it continued to attract, during that time, a public fascinated by the anomalous. After the age of the fair came the circus, of which P. T. Barnum's American Big Top was the most successful. The travelling circus continued to present to the public a range of human curiosities, perhaps the most famous of whom was General Tom Thumb, born Charles Sherwood Stratton in Connecticut in 1838. For his lifetime, Tom Thumb stood only twenty-five inches high and weighed sixteen pounds. Under the management of P. T. Barnum, Tom Thumb went on several exhibition tours of Europe and gave royal command performances. He was a magnetic attraction and brought tens of thousands of people into Barnum's Big Top. The substantial wealth he accumulated during his lifetime testified to the fascination of the human anomaly.

The nineteenth-century novelist Victor Hugo (1887) described the streets of the nineteenth-century European city as peopled with a literal army of deformed beggars and tricksters who performed in order to gain favours from a deceived bourgeoisie. Many of these stigmatized individuals were deliberately misshapen in order to elicit sympathy and be regarded as toys who could be purchased for entertainment: 'in order that a human toy should prove a success, he must be taken in hand early. The dwarf must be fashioned when young ... Hence grew an art. There were trainers who took a man and made him an abortion; they took a face and made a muzzle; they stunted growth: they distorted the features. The artificial production of teratological cases had its rules. It was quite a science.' Such practices have continued into the twentieth century. Mahfouz, the 1988 Nobel Prize winner in literature, has written of the 'cripple-maker', Ziata, in his book *Midaq Alley* (1947): 'People came to him who wanted to become beggars, and with his extraordinary craft ... he would cripple each customer in a manner appropriate to his body. They came to him whole, and left hunchbacked, pigeon-breasted, or with arms and legs cut off short.'

Early views of congenital human defectives referred to them as *lusus naturae*, jokes of nature. Aristotle had depicted them as the result of too much or too little seed, or the susceptibility of women to vivid impressions made by frightening and hideous sights, or from their mating with lower animals. As ludicrous creatures, Aristotle considered it perfectly acceptable that the physically deformed be regarded as a sub-human species and displayed in public for profit and amusement, or that they be kept for one's own pleasure as household pets.

Cave drawings and wood carvings depicting individuals with two heads or three arms or a taliped, suggest an early interest in human anomalies. Ancient Babylonian clay tablets record in cuneiform a wide range of congenital malformations. To some extent, this interest may have been prompted by a belief in augury and the popular practices of foetomancy, that is, prophecy by means of studying foetuses, and teratoscopy which was divination based on the examination of abnormal births. Births of malformed human beings were omens; an infant born with no fingers foretold of no further births in the local populace, and an infant with no nostrils meant the ruination of the family (Warkany 1959).

This long history of interest in the human anomaly is also recorded in early medical treatises. In 1573 Ambroise Paré (1510–90), a French barber-surgeon of considerable prestige who had ministered to Henry II, Francis II and Charles IX, provided a partial list of the most common causes of human anomalies, known in the vernacular as monsters. These were not deliberately manufactured, as Hugo, Mahfouz and Kunzle were to document three and four centuries later, but were accidents of nature or attributed to the anomalous individual's unnatural desires and circumstances. Paré specified ten conditions which produced human defects; these included fate, God's will and the general conduct of women. Individuals who suffered from diseases such as leprosy, scurvy, gout, smallpox and measles were thought to have been conceived during their mother's menstruation. Often, monstrous infants were thought to result from the mother's misconduct; for instance, if the pregnant woman had an 'indecent posture', if she sat for too long in the 'unnatural position of her legs crossed', then a concomitant form of damage would be conveyed to the infant *in utero*. Or, if she had a vivid imagination, her thoughts and impressions were conveyed to the infant and translated into physical deformities. As well, if the woman were promiscuous and 'seed was mixed and mingled within her', then a deformed child would result (Paré 1982:3–4).

The first extant treatise on human teratoses has been dated to the sixth century and attributed to Isidore of Seville (Sharpe 1964). However, the formal codification of teratology is most often associated with the work of Etienne Geoffroy Saint-Hilaire (1772–1844) and his son Isidore. Saint-Hilaire, the elder, conducted experiments on animals, fish and insects in order to produce terata from the effects of external physical agents such as abnormal atmosphere, nutritional deficiencies and the mutilation of the embryo. As a result, Saint-Hilaire could argue that physical abnormalities resulted from an arrest in the normal development, or an interruption in the sequence of growth, and it was this which created the anomaly. Earlier, William Harvey, better known for his theory of the circulation of blood (which, when published in 1651, in effect, brought to a close the fifteen-hundred-year influence of Galenic humoural theory) had described the aetiology of the cleft lip and palate, known popularly as a harelip. According to Harvey, this mal-formation resulted from the arrested development of the foetus at that equivalent stage of maturation which produced a hare, deer, cow and other resemblant animals sharing this particular lip and mouth formation. The principle underlying the theory was that ontogeny recapitulated phylogeny, that is, each embryo developed step by step through the stages of the lower animals – a biological theory which would not be articulated as such until the nineteenth century. In the seventeenth century, the explanation of individuals with physical abnormalities was attributed to their arrested foetal development; such individuals were at a lower stage of development comparable to the animal, bird or insect which they resembled.

Over the centuries, the different explanations of human ano-malies have been variously couched in supernatural, fantastic and mythical terms. Some explanations implicated devils, spir-its and divine intermediaries such as centaurs, minotaurs and satyrs. In 1493 that eminent figure in the origins of modern medicine, Paracelsus, used a hybrid theory of human anomalies to account for the fantastic creature, the basilisk, a combination cock and toad. Such a fantastic creature was a warning of what would result from unnatural human desires and acts. Another medical authority, Pierre Boaistuau, in 1560, similarly ex-plained the prodigy, an imaginary half-man half-animal, with reference to other-worldly forces. These early theories of hu-man teratology and their fantastic views of the malformed have not altogether receded into obscurity as may be expected, but have persisted throughout the centuries to have resonances in some modern perspectives. For example, associated with certain religious orthodoxies is the belief that those with physical deformities are the product of individuals who have sinned or transgressed against fundamental laws of God or nature.

A most enduring explanation of human malformations has been that of 'maternal impressions'. Aristotle, Paracelsus, Paré and Descartes each considered that human defects were the result of frightening and horrible events to which pregnant women were exposed. It was thought that horrible sights could impress themselves so strongly upon pregnant women that the face and the body of the foetus would absorb these horrors and be transmogrified. For example, women who looked at monkeys could give birth to microcephalic infants (Warkany 1959). In *The Hunchback of Notre Dame* (1831) Victor Hugo has given an account of this widespread belief. In this story, pregnant women were warned that looking at the deformed Quasimodo was to risk their unborn child being misshapen by maternal impressions (Hugo 1831:16). Another allusion to the impression theory is the case of John Merrick, the elephant man, whose neurofibromatosis was attributed to an unspecified trauma suffered by his mother. Keating's nineteenth-century *Encyclopaedia of Diseases in Children* (1889) reported a further ninety instances of human malformations which could be caused by maternal impressions. Montaigne's sixteenth-century essay, *On the Power of the Imagination* (see Hazlitt 1892), stated that 'we know by experience that women impart the marks of their fancy to the bodies of the children they carry in their womb.' In short, it was often seen to be the fault of pregnant women that human defects were produced.

After the sixteenth century a little more attention came to be paid to the mechanical conditions of pregnancy as probable causes of human malformations. When the uterus was too narrow, or the pregnant woman displayed poor posture, or pressures caused by amniotic fluids in the womb were detected, then an abnormal infant was expected. Where there was scoliosis (a curvature of the spine), or talipes (a club foot), or a hemiplegia, (paralysis on one side of the body), the mechanics of pregnancy were cited as the cause. In the eighteenth century combinations of causes were postulated; Watson (1749) argued that *in utero* diseases along with the faulty implantation of seed could produce a malformed human. In the burgeoning scientific culture of the nineteenth century accounts of human oddities, superstitions and fantastic theories were mentioned less frequently, and more emphasis was placed upon formal medical and scientific knowledge. Slowly it became accepted that genetic endowment, disease and poor nutrition may well be important teratogens (Barrow 1971). In the twentieth century the history of the causes of human defects is still being written. The aetiology of certain conditions remains uncertain, or so amorphous that few predisposing elements can be identified. For example, Cornelia de Lange syndrome, congenital hypothyroidism and Prader-Willi syndrome continue to be largely inexplicable as do more common conditions such as autism and many instances of cerebral palsy. As well, exogenous factors such as industrial pollution and the use of licit and illicit drugs may be suspected of being teratogens but have not been officially acknowledged as such. Nor, similarly, have concerted efforts been made to prevent foetal damage by enshrining in law specific regulatory practices such as those governing food preparations and environmental pollution from industrial wastes. In short, the physical conditions which give rise to the teratogen are still being mapped.

In sharp contrast, the social causes of stigma are well enough known and, surprisingly, despite a prominent medical presence in modern society and a supposedly more enlightened view of human differences, the social origins remain consonant with archaic fantasies and old beliefs. It is more commonly the social relations of exploitation, degradation and ostracism which marginalize the physically different, and not their actual physical attributes. For example, the dwarf has been the object of exploitation for centuries. Irrespective of whether the condition was caused by rickets, chondrodystrophy, achondroplasia or Kashin-Beck's disease, the social ostracism of the dwarf has not much altered. Such individuals who have been known as 'gente de placer', an amusement for the bored, have been variously exploited for profit or service, and have been used as mascots, portents and victims throughout the centuries. Dwarfs were used in the gladitorial arenas of ancient Rome. The Romans distinguished natural dwarfs, *nanus*, from those manufactured by starvation or confinement in small jars or cages, *pumilo*. Mark Antony has been attributed with ownership of a dwarf named Sisyphus; Attila the Hun was described by Priscus of Panium as being a dwarf because of his squat body, large head and flat nose; Catherine de' Medici was said to have included five dwarfs in her retinue – Majowski, Merlin, Mandricart, Pelauine and Rodomont (Thompson 1930; Roth and Comie 1968; Truzzi 1968; *Chambers Biographical Dictionary* 1969).

The long-lived awe of the human oddity has been preserved by art as much as it has by commercial exploitation. Dwarfs have been prominent in paintings, for example, those of Brueghel in the sixteenth century, Van Dyck and Velàzquez in the seventeenth century and Goya in the eighteenth century. In the twentieth century, dwarfs have been exploited in advertising for such products as Oscar Mayer Smallgoods, Buster Brown shoes and Sunshine baked goods. They have regularly featured in money-spinning and exhibitionist spectator sports such as wrestling and weightlifting, and in popular films and television series for prurient and entertainment value. The fascination that human anomalies have held throughout history and their susceptibility to commercial exploitation are difficult phenomena to explain; however, it is clear that their histories reflect widely held assumptions that the physically anomalous are extraordinary, outside the bounds of normalcy and, so, lesser beings. These attitudes and values, which underpin stigma, encourage an exploitative commerce in human difference which seems to be deeply embedded in the culture of the everyday.

The presence of the monstrous in art and literature gives some indication of the intellectual substratum underlying our categorization of people by their appearance and, in particular, the characterization of some physical defects as emblems of evil. Duby (1988b:509–34) and Régnier-Bohler (1988:313) accept that literature is not a mirror of the social reality, but it does reveal much about the relationship between the individual and the collectivity. Nineteenth-century literature is replete with descriptions of the physically deformed and curious, for example, Mary Shelley's *Frankenstein* (1818) and Victor Hugo's *The Hunchback of Notre Dame* (1831). From this period, the topic of the humanly monstrous seems to have entered regularly into popular literary forms. There has followed a parade of odd characters such as those found in *The Old Curiosity Shop* (1841) by Charles Dickens, *Tales of the Grotesque* (1847) by Edgar Allan Poe, *Dr Jekyll and Mr Hyde* (1886) by Robert Louis Stevenson, and into the twentieth century, we find *Memoirs of a Midget* (1921) by Walter de la Mare, *Nightwood* (1936) by Djuna Barnes and the short fiction, *Scenes from the Life of a Double Monster* (1958), Vladimir Nabokov's account of the Siamese twins Chang and Eng. As well, in the late twentieth century, we have dozens of examples of the human monstrosity in the popular horror film. Without obvious exception, these individuals are deemed to be lesser and inferior beings who cannot make the same claims upon the society as can other citizens.

Mary Shelley's *Frankenstein* was subtitled 'The Modern Prometheus'. Its protagonist, Victor Frankenstein, succeeded in bringing life to inanimate matter. Frankenstein developed his monster from a study of the chimerical truths of ancient science (Shelley 1967:24–7) and, in so doing, resembled the Greek legendary hero Prometheus who stole the secret of life from the gods. In the tale of *Frankenstein*, the ancient message that knowledge is the precursor of tragedy is being retold. The gods' secret of bestowing life had been stolen and applied to the making of the creature. Shelley used the monster as a metaphor of the new science of the industrial age and as a warning of future hubris. In the story, the pursuit of knowledge is depicted as being an humanitarian and benign enterprise which, at the same time, can also be pirated and misappropriated. Shelley remonstrated that human history has been fraught with instances of such misappropriations in which the ideals of science are too easily sullied by the ambitions of those who are expedient and utilitarian. Thus, while a scientist such as Victor Frankenstein may be impelled in his pursuits by noble intentions, others may not. Frankenstein's created monster was a scientific wonder, but before any benefits could be gleaned from it, the natural brutality of the humans who encountered the anomaly unwittingly caused the monster to become vengeful and malicious. The monster says of himself, 'my

2 Refining Appearance, Improving Character

heart was fashioned to be susceptible of love and sympathy'
(1967:192). 'I was benevolent and good' (1967:84) he states,
but, when others saw him as 'a vile insect' and a 'wretched
devil' (1967:83), then he came to see himself as they did, as an
exile and outcast: 'all men hate the wretched' (1967:83), 'I
retreated ... from the barbarity of man' (1967:91).

The creature was rejected because of his awesome appearance. Even Victor Frankenstein, who presumably watched the
figure take shape, was 'unable to endure the aspect of the being
I had created' (1967:42), 'its unearthly ugliness (was) too horrible for human eyes' (1967:83). Yet the monster knew nothing
of his appearance until others treated him as monstrous
(1967:99), and it was through his social ostracism that he
became malevolently monstrous.

His yellow skin scarcely covered the work of muscles and arter-
ies beneath; his hair was of a lustrous black, and flowing; his
teeth of a pearly whiteness; but these luxuriances only formed a
more horrid contrast with his watery eyes, that seemed almost
of the same colour as the dun-white sockets in which they were
set, his shrivelled complexion and straight black lips ... No
mortal could support the horror of that countenance. A mummy
again endued with animation could not be so hideous as that
wretch ... when those muscles and joints were rendered capable of motion it became a thing such as even Dante could not
have conceived. (1967:42-3)

In these descriptions, an association between the creature's
appearance and his character is pointedly made. He was shunned and exiled before he actually engaged others; his grotesque
face and body were sufficient to earn him the appellation of
monster. The creature soon understood the unjust principle
which caused him to be excluded from society and, for one
moment, he was able to convince Victor of its injustice. Almost
immediately, though, Victor was swayed back by the gruesome
appearance of his supplicant; 'when I looked upon him, when I
saw the filthy mass that moved and talked, my heart sickened
and my feelings were altered to those of horror and hatred'
(1967:132). 'His soul is as hellish as his form, full of treachery
and fiendlike malice' (1967:192).

61

Shelley's story well illustrates the fate of any hapless individual who falls beyond the limits of tolerance. Being socially rejected makes the individual more monstrous. As Frankenstein's unnamed creature lamented, 'I am malicious because I am miserable. Am I not shunned and hated by all mankind?' (1967:130) 'I, the miserable and abandoned, am an abortion, to be spurned at, and kicked, and trampled on' (1967:204). But, he added moralistically, 'Am I to be thought the only criminal when all mankind sinned against me?' (1967:204).

The fate of Quasimodo, Victor Hugo's fictional inhabitant of Notre Dame, was similar to that of Shelley's creature. Quasimodo was as repellent to humans as was Frankenstein's monster. He was 'one-eyed, hunchbacked and bow-legged', 'only an approximation of a human being' (Hugo 1831:59). In the fictive universe of nineteenth-century Paris, Quasimodo was deemed monstrous and a portent of evil when, as an infant, he was found deposited on the steps of Notre Dame Cathedral, his disfigurements were already visible and many thought that he should have been immediately destroyed – either drowned or burned (1831:54). He was saved by his future guardian, the archdeacon of Notre Dame, Claude Frollo, who kept him in private service and exploited him as a slave. Like Frankenstein's monster, Quasimodo repelled others who then mocked and insulted him (1831:61), and such treatment made him hateful (1831:27). His attempts to act like others and to pursue the same pleasures only intensified their vilification. So it was when Quasimodo became infatuated with the gypsy, La Esmeralda; it was not only his appearance which made the romantic alliance seem ridiculous, but also the presumption that he possessed an inner character much like others and could experience love as they did. Although, Quasimodo treated Esmeralda with greater kindness than any of her other suitors, including the priestly Claude Frollo, it made no difference: Quasimodo was a monster and his desires for Esmeralda were an affront. He was to be reviled, his physical abnormalities made him less than human and were regarded as obstacles to his moral and intellectual development. His misshapen physical form was taken as a measure of his character; as he looked so he was.

The morality embedded in these tales show the inaccuracy or at least injustice of drawing an association between physical appearance and character. Frankenstein's creature and Quasimodo came to act in monstrous ways, not because of any inherent wickedness but because of the persecution and inhumanity meted out to them by the acceptable members of society. The morality of these tales is that the origins of the monstrous lies not in the supernatural but within the ordinary capacities of each of us. Robert Louis Stevenson's *Dr Jekyll and Mr Hyde* (1886) well illustrates the case.

Dr Jekyll was a handsome and outstandingly elegant member of the professional upper classes. By his attractive physical bearing he exuded a character of honesty and gentility. From his appearance one would never know that he harboured a secret desire to unleash a darker side of his nature. The tumult of selfishness and greed that lay dormant in the internal reservoir of his character, could only be tapped when the outward persona was made into their reflection – thus, appearance must coincide with character. So, Jekyll struggled with the mysteries of human chemistry in order to alter himself. After much experimentation, Jekyll was finally successful and he unleashed the wizened, monstrous Hyde from his interior world. It was as if Hyde resided on the other side of a membranous divide between normalcy and the submerged universe of character. He was barely concealed, as Stevenson has described, behind 'the trembling immateriality the mist-like transcience of this seemingly so solid body in which we walk attired' (Stevenson 1886:82). Hyde's appearance had the same effect of previous monsters, namely, that of conjuring up a sense of imbalance and menace. His physiognomy was enough to suggest disorder; 'Mr Hyde was pale and dwarfish; he gave the impression of deformity without any nameable malformation', and as a result, 'the man seems hardly human. Something troglodytic' (1886:40). He was a herald of the new experimental age where 'scientific heresies' and 'scientific balderdash' (1886:36) held the possibility of unleashing the unexpected and disturbing.

In *Dr Jekyll and Mr Hyde* there is a symbiotic portrayal of the extraordinary and ordinary. Jekyll and Hyde are the inversion of each other, and as such the suggestion is that every representation of the ordinary and acceptable can transmogrify, in the right circumstances – and, as Goffman would have it – into its opposite, namely, the awesome and repellent. Thus, the depths of Hyde's depravity are held in suspension by the divertingly benign appearance of the good doctor, Jekyll. The mutualism of depravity and goodness are similarly depicted in the relationship of Frankenstein's monster with his creator. It is as if the vengefulness of the monster corresponded in intensity with Frankenstein's eager pursuit of his scientific desires. The same mutuality existed between Quasimodo and his tormentors. Quasimodo's ludicrousness was a measure of how laughable others found him. The moral tale is clear: the origins of the monstrous lie with those who live in dread of the extraordinary. The greedy, depraved Hyde is a spectre of our own imagination. The darker side of reality we imagine he inhabits is made into an underworld. The narrative is instructing us that evil resides only in the other, over there, and not in ourselves. The twinning of the degenerate Hyde with the elegant Jekyll personifies the dual, parallel worlds of the normal and the aberrant: 'it was the curse of mankind that these incongruous faggots were thus bound together – that in the agonised womb of consciousness these polar twins should be continuously struggling' (Stevenson 1886:82).

In the imaginative realms of literature, the responses of fear, revulsion and intolerance shown toward the human anomaly are copiously represented. There, the physically anomalous individual has been repeatedly depicted as dangerous, evil, beguiling and mischievous; s/he has the capacity to threaten the status quo, to travel beyond the horizons of the normal and acceptable into the disquietening realms of the unpredictable and disorderly. The unaccountable origins of these mutant individuals suggest that they can appear at any time and, in this way, the mystery and threat of being stigmatized are intensified.

Fiedler (1981) has argued that travesties of the human form hold immense subconscious appeal, and that throughout the ages and across cultures, people have been irrepressibly drawn to look upon them. The mutant individual is disturbingly different yet retains an obvious closeness with the human form.

As such, s/he functions to delineate the normative limits of the self. Fiedler has accounted for the lure of the anomalous by making it a mockery of the human condition; it is as if we harboured a secret self, an immersed, repressed side of our nature, of which we live in fear because it could, at any time, burst from us unaccountably and, in so doing, instantly propel us beyond the boundaries of the acceptable. This idea has much in common with the claims of the physiognomists. They had argued for the importance of scrutinizing the physical appearance of the other, of analysing each element of conduct and appearance in order to be aware of the concealed attributes of character and the hidden dimensions of the self. It is an idea that also had currency in the emergence of contemporary manners and our styles of conduct in the modern city populated with strangers.

Sennett's analysis of the styles of public demeanour in eighteenth- and nineteenth-century society has shown how pervasive was the physiognomic perspective and how much reliance was placed on appearances. Sennett has decribed how physical appearance and dress codes, in particular, were important because the least incongruity in appearance could be detected as a tell-tale detail that warned others of a lurking barbarity, a monstrous self only partially contained, which could erupt into society and destroy the fabric of civilization. Thus, the manner of one's public demeanour was interpreted by others as a signal that one's incipient incivility was being kept effectively under control. The fragile boundary between civility and the social chaos of an unleashed inner character was thought to be as fine and subtle as the buttons on a coat, the fabric of trousers or dress, the quality of boot leather and the cleanliness of a neckband (Sennett 1976:165–6). 'People took each other's appearances in the street immensely seriously; they believed they could fathom the character of those they saw . . . Finding out about a person from how he or she looked became, therefore, a matter of looking for clues in the details of his costume' (Sennett 1976:161). Clothes represented psychological symbols and appearance revealed states of personal feeling.

As character and personality were regarded as immanent in appearance, and as these signs of character could be as esoteric as the quality of one's boot leather, then one's perception of the other needed to be extremely acute. Sennett has given the example of how a gentleman is proved as such because he does not make the claim to be one: 'a gentleman disclosed his quality only to those who had the knowledge to perceive it without being told ... one could always recognize gentlemanly dress because the buttons on the sleeves of a gentleman's coat actually buttoned and unbuttoned, while one recognized gentlemanly behavior in his keeping the buttons scrupulously fastened, so that his sleeves never called attention to this fact' (Sennett 1976:166).

The belief that character was immanent in appearance has been crucially important in the formulation of modern social manners. In support of the contention, Sennett has quoted the famous fictional detective Sherlock Holmes on the 'importance of sleeves, the suggestiveness of thumbnails, (and) the great issues that may hang from a boot-lace' (Conan Doyle in Sennett 1976:169). The growing concern with the details of dress, speech and performance, shown by the eighteenth- and nineteenth-century bourgeoisie also produced a parallel concern with the control of personal appearance and style of conduct as the means for protecting oneself from the penetrative eye of the other. Sennett has maintained that the belief in the involuntary disclosure of character through one's appearance and conduct produced a new type of self-consciousness and anxiety that, in turn, heightened the desire to anticipate the responses of others to one's own behaviour (Sennett 1976:168). In order to control the clues by which others read one's personality, the individual became skilful in deflecting the others' gaze. One's style in clothing and demeanour were employed as techniques to control the opinions of others. Goffman (1963) has recognized this same manner of sociality in the twentieth-century practice of 'impression management'.

When an ethic of bodily awareness exists and distinctions between individuals are strongly asserted irrespective of their facticity, then a rampant self-consciousness and anxiety over physical appearance can be seen as the authenticating narrative of the time. In such an atmosphere, the process of refining physical appearance is simultaneously an exercise in shaping character. Why else, we must ask, is the desire to control physical appearance, through fashionable dress, exercise, diet and the use of cosmetics, so prevalent and strong? A sense of the necessity to regulate appearances and to police the extraordinary has been a striking motif of the modern era. Foucault's (1977; 1980) analyses of regulatory social institutions well illustrate how any suggestions of aberration or challenges to the prevailing norms need to be ostentatiously converted into more understandable, that is, 'normal' phenomena. Any examples of physical aberration could not remain as anomalies or polymorphic examples of the human form; instead, they had to be redefined into instances of illness, criminality, physical monstrosity and so on. Often, this was done by the application of a scientistic, rationalistic narrative. Foucault has defined this propensity to control as the signature of modernity and has located its power with the professional echelons of the emerging modern state where assessment tools have been developed for the hierarchical evaluation of the modern individual.

In most cultures the human body has been regarded as a material asset. In subsistence societies it may be seen as a tool for the production of food and communal survival; in a competitive, industrialized society it may be the means by which social status and power are symbolically represented to others. When the body diverges from the norm, when it exhibits eccentric proportions, uncontrolled movements, atrophy, atonia or asymmetry, it becomes a traitor to social rules. The aberrant individual will be responded to differently and will be judged in comparison with the limits of the normative order. This is the character of the era in which we live. It is not surprising then that ample opportunity exists for the modification of physical appearance. We can fashion ourselves anew with clothes, cosmetics, diet, exercise and plastic surgery. The question which these possibilities prompt is, does our ability to alter physical appearance, to some extent at whim, undermine the idea that character can be read from appearance?

The same question about the relationship between appearances and reality was asked in the nineteenth century when the theatre of realism became popular. In this context, the question of the relationship between appearance and character took the form of asking whether the stage actor was truly representing the emotions and experiences of the individual when it was understood that s/he was not actually living out the drama but was only re-creating it, within the confines of a theatrical performance. The question posed the problem of whether a performance could be true (Sennett 1976:109–15). In a similar way, when we don an outfit of clothing, when we follow the tacit rules of sociation, when we deliberately reshape ourselves by diet, exercise or surgery, or when we imitate certain styles of conduct, the question of authenticity appears – by these efforts are we revealing our character or concealing it?

In the consumer culture of the modern society, physical appearance has come to be seen as an important means for claiming a degree of social status. The industries which commodify the human body are new industries; they offer fashioned and designer styles in mass-produced clothing, individualized fitness programmes, exercise equipment for home use, private gymnasiums and diet regimens. They also provide medical and surgical procedures, including a variety of cosmetic surgery. These techniques and procedures are the means by which a new personality, a refinement of character and a better identity are thought to be moulded. The availability of these goods and services indicates an ethos in which physical appearance is held to be of paramount importance. The body, like other consumer objects which represent prestige and status, has been transformed into a sign, a material commodity (see Lasch 1979; Featherstone 1987). As Morgenthau and Person (1978:347) have described, the contemporary individual experiences his or her own body as distinctive from all others; thus, it 'becomes the ultimate reality of attention, nurturance and care, hence the proliferation of institutes for body culture and cultist attempts at gaining heightened consciousness through cultivation of the body.'

The argument presented here is that the physiognomic principle of the detection of character from outward physical signs remains an axiom of sociality in modern times. The puzzle is that the idea still holds sway, even though techniques for fashioning the body abound. In the modern era, moral entrepreneurs, such as technocrats, scientists and doctors, are able to exercise authority through designating which individuals are normal and which are aberrant, and to provide therapeutic or remedial services to correct any detected deficiencies and inadequacies. The increasingly detailed notation of correctible human features is a reflection of the proliferation of techniques now available with which to alter and presumably refine appearance. These mechanisms and services are available not because modern individuals are inherently more flawed, but because the belief in physical appearance as a signpost to human character has not been expunged from our culture. Indeed, if we consider the growth in the 'body industries', including the development of modern medicine, the possibility emerges that the belief in character as immanent in appearance has intensified.

To consider the practice of medicine and its allied professions as part of a body industry is to consider that the efficacy of modern medicine is much concerned with its ability to effect an improvement in the individuals social functioning. Bunker (1985) has claimed that the practice of medicine does not, in the main, save us from life-threatening conditions but, in the long term, serves to ensure our better adaptation to social prescriptions of proper conduct and performance. That is, medical treatments can act to regulate social conduct and improve the individual's social standing (see also Illich 1975; Taylor 1979; Kennedy 1981). In cases where individuals have physical anomalies, it would seem to be irrelevant whether the source of the individual's anomalous appearance is trauma, a congenital condition or an iatrogenic legacy. The same pressures for homogenizing appearance and reshaping the body to approximate the cultural norm are still at work. Medical expertise is readily available for that task.

The ethics of modern medicine become increasingly equivocal as the profession's accomplishments multiply. In the instance of human abnormality, medicine can respond well to the needs of damaged people by correcting or relieving certain disabling conditions. At the same time, if physical appearances were less important, then the activities of medicine could be applied elsewhere. However, at present, the profession of medicine is generously applied to fashioning physical appearances and, in this way, works as an agent in the production of the stigma that it then attempts to correct. That is, the modern physician defines which physical conditions are anomalous, deleterious and undesirable, and which conditions are suitable for therapeutic intervention. The employment of medicine as an arbiter in defining instances of human anomaly is itself a strategy by which certain individuals are socially marginalized. Often, this can be in a literal sense, as medical opinion becomes the basis for re-locating the physically different and disabled into institutions and sequestered living environments, literally and figuratively at the margins of society. The profession of medicine helps maintain a cultural homogeneity and it does so by assisting us to avoid, in our everyday activities, any encounters with examples of human diversity which would otherwise require of us a greater degree of tolerance and civility.

Having the power to define the human anomaly has served the interests of the medical profession by creating a field of subjects and supplicants. Historically, the advance of modern medicine has required the opportunity for experimentation (Waddington 1973; Jewson 1976); therefore, the existence of a population upon whom medical experimentation can take place has been invaluable for the advance of the profession. The physically anomalous and disabled have provided the experimental subjects. They have frequently been the recipients of experimentation in surgical techniques, diagnostics and therapeutics. Even in the case of the new-born, this has occurred. Duff and Campbell (1973:890–4; 1979:187–208) have shown that physicians are reluctant to leave new-born defective infants without treatment or aggressive management because in so doing they lose the opportunity to practise new medical skills and techniques; in addition, they waste an opportunity for didactic demonstration of procedures to medical students.

This illustrates a major dilemma of modern medicine; while medical procedures can intervene to alter the appearance of certain human anomalies, it may be the case that such interventions have only cosmetic and little or no therapeutic value. So, in modifying the appearance of the physically distinctive individual, medicine is acting simultaneously to reinforce and perpetuate expressions of social intolerance toward those who are anomalous in some way. For example, the individual with Down's syndrome has a characteristic appearance which includes macroglossia or an enlarged tongue. The tongue keeps the mouth open, increases drooling and can distort other facial features such as the nose. Furthermore, the uncontrollable muscular thrusting of the tongue can make speech and eating more difficult. Macroglossia is an aesthetically displeasing physical feature and those suffering it are stigmatized. A recent surgical procedure known as a partial glossectomy, removes a wedge of muscle from the mid-section of the tongue, thereby reducing its size. While it was hoped that this surgery would have therapeutic value, to date no studies have confirmed a significant improvement in the speech or feeding patterns of the individual (Parsons et al. 1987; American Foundation for Craniofacial Deformities n.d.). The most acclaimed result of the surgery is the improved appearance of the individual.

Other characteristic features of Down's syndrome, such as the flattened nose, slanted eyes and fatty deposits above and below the eyes, can also be altered with surgery. Bone grafts can be used to build up the nose, and the eyes can be reshaped by the excision of fatty deposits in the surrounding tissue. Such surgery exacts a toll; it takes several hours to perform, requires hospitalization and a two- or three-week period of recuperation. The information on Down's syndrome published by the American Foundation for Craniofacial Deformities contains the statement that 'many times, surgery will not achieve the kind of dramatic result one would expect.' This statement appears above a large full-face photograph of a young girl with Down's syndrome. She is blonde, neatly dressed and has a conventionally attractive appearance. The facial characteristics of Down's syndrome are, in her case, minimal. The ambiguity of the statement is clear; surgical procedures are available and should be used to give as normal an appearance as possible; however, surgery may not satisfy the expectation of a marked change in the individual's social acceptability.

The equivocation of the medical profession rests with the problem that, on the one hand, the abnormal individual can profit socially if not therapeutically from surgery because altering appearance can mitigate and help avoid the general intoler-

71

ance of the community toward physical aberrations. On the other hand, surgical interventions which attempt to 'normalize' appearance may only intensify the sense of being a social liability when appearance proves intractable. The American Foundation for Craniofacial Deformities has resolved this dilemma by stating that surgery is justifiable even if the results are measurable only in social and not therapeutic terms. For example, in the case of combined physical and intellectual disability:

> Most physicians and health care professionals do not view surgery as necessary for any individual with impaired mental functioning. *We, on the other hand, believe that mental retardation in and of itself does not constitute an adequate justification for denying any patient the opportunity for surgical reconstruction and perhaps improved acceptance by our society.* Our preliminary psychosocial studies suggest the potential for increases in both intellectual and psychosocial functioning in children who have undergone reconstructive plastic surgery based on improved self esteem and peer popularity. *Many times the stigma of a deformity – Down's Syndrome or other – is more crippling than the actual physical manifestations of the disease entity.* (original emphases)

Surgical procedures may be undertaken just because the techniques and opportunities are available and not because an improved outcome is assured. This is often the case with cosmetic and non-therapeutic surgery. The actions of the medical practitioner in correcting the anomalous features of the individual must be juxtaposed with the question of whose interests are being better served. Will the surgical treatment be so effective that the anomalous individual will be re-absorbed into society? Will community attitudes of intolerance toward different appearances be reduced or, perhaps, heightened as fewer stigmatized individuals remain visible in the community? Are the professional interests of the medical and therapeutic team being advanced inappropriately by treatment of all kinds of human anomaly?

When a defective infant is born, parents often experience guilt, a sense of failure and a rejection of the child (Giannini and Goodman 1963:743–4; Kennell and Klaus 1971:928–40; Walker *et al.* 1971:462–76). Ariès (1962:413) has argued, in a historical study of the European family, that in the modern era, the child has become a representation of adult claims for social status. The married, reproductive individual has greater social value than the single individual. However, when there is a birth of an imperfect child, the contribution of the parents to the society may not be so clear and their claims for social status may thereby be jeopardized. Subsequently, the parents of a physically damaged child may seek surgical treatment as a means of altering the child's appearance in order to gain some degree of social acceptability. For other contrasting reasons, the medical practitioner may wish to perform the surgery for professional self-interest, irrespective of the prognosis and outcome. In many instances, individuals with disabling and disfiguring conditions do receive relief from surgical procedures, but, at the same time, a long history of medical abuse has been visited upon the disabled, subnormal and incarcerated without necessarily producing important enough results to offset or justify such an iniquitous history (Pappworth 1969; Rice 1988). It must be considered, that embedded in every successful remediation of a stigmatizing condition, there is a hidden history of experimentation and iatrogenic failure, and the individuals involved may subsequently emerge from the therapeutic world worse off than before.

Social awareness of the personal problems associated with physical disability has greatly increased in recent decades. The financial contributions to welfare programmes from both the private and public sectors have significantly increased. Physically disabled individuals have forged political pressure groups to improve their own circumstances. The politicizing of the disabled as a socially marginalized and disadvantaged group has improved the living and working conditions of these individuals to the extent that, now, some degree of social equality is enjoyed. Better public education and the greater availability of community services have contributed to the demystification of the disabled person. As well as a heightened visibility, there are also increased numbers of people with disabilities due to improvements in medical techniques and health management, both in the early stages of life, and through into adulthood. For example, those with cerebral palsy, spina bifida and other congenital deformities are surviving infancy and remaining alive in the community for much longer than in previous times (see Lorber 1974:307–8; Colen 1976).

At first sight, these social changes may be explained as characteristic of any liberal and affluent community which has a more elaborated cultural base from which can emerge a greater tolerance of human differences. However, in a society where physical beauty and prowess are highly valued and where elective cosmetic surgery has become increasingly commonplace, it is important to consider the ethics of providing non-therapeutic surgery to those with physical anomalies. Medicine, at this point, can readily become self-serving; it can stigmatize and medicalize those particular physical conditions which it can then service. In this way, the medical practitioner gains economically and professionally by ensuring a demand for services which, at the same time, provide the didactic experiences by which the profession trains its members and improves its services.

During the second half of this century, the sense of fear and outrage evoked by the sight of a physically deformed person, who in previous centuries would be called monstrous, has been greatly modified. The application of techniques to conceal human frailties and disabilities, through the use of prostheses, corrective surgery and such, has been significant in changing attitudes. Nonetheless, this is an age where human perfectibility is valued and where the tacit promises of medical practice are understood to be the improvement if not perfection of the human body. In such an era, individuals who are physically different are made acutely aware of their distinctiveness, and the stigmatizing of an anomalous individual is not always the benign precursor to that individual's being successfully remediated by modern medical techniques. It is not a straightforward matter that the anomalous individual becomes aware of his or her difference and is then successfully treated by the medical profession. The generalized cultural value assigned to human perfectibility and physical attractiveness, which draws from a bedrock of physiognomic assumptions about character being immanent in appearance, helps to create a perpetual demand for improvements and changes in appearance. This is certainly the current situation where demand for the treatment of various physical conditions does not always come from those individuals in need of therapeutic help. The conditions to be corrected are not, in any physiological or historical sense, monstrous or anomalous.

The availability of medical treatments does not guarantee their delivery to those individuals in most need, nor does it mean that these practices are successful in reducing the sources of social stigma. Thus, the contemporary employment of medical strategies in the management of stigma cannot automatically be taken as a sign of a cultural desire to eradicate stigma, nor as an effective means to bring about a reduction in social intolerance toward physically distinctive individuals. For instance, the increasing availability of cosmetic and non-therapeutic surgical techniques and the nascent industries of genetic and somatic therapies are activities which are fuelled by a growing popular interest and desire to eradicate all possible instances of physical aberration or anomaly whether these are disabling or not (Stanworth 1987; Meredith 1988). After all, in this technologically sophisticated society the question can be asked why should appearances be allowed to miscast the individual when opportunities exist to alter one's appearance through reconstructive surgery? The emphasis appears to be: why not remodel those tell-tale physical signs which can adversely influence others' opinions of us, why continue to be unjustly disadvantaged by them? Undergirding this imperialism of appearance are assumptions continuous with those of the physiognomists, especially those which locate the truth of character in physical appearance.

The individual of uncommon proportions or uncontrolled movements inadvertently brings attention to the value placed upon a conventional human form. When individuals fail to meet these expectations, they are excluded from the mainstream and assigned to a secondary social universe from which little of value is expected to emanate. Consequently, the avoidance of physical stigma becomes a social dynamic, and individuals may take extraordinary measures to avoid being physically distinctive. In this way, appearance becomes endowed with imperialistic and dictatorial powers; individuals of all shapes and sizes will come to view themselves as being in need of correctives and therapies to alter their appearance so that they better approximate the prevailing ideals. In a society based upon material competition and status inequality, where a sense of personal satisfaction must always be lacking in order to promote competition and desire, the emphasis placed upon appearance and the stigmatizing of various physical features has the effect of encouraging an insatiable appetite for alternatives and changes to one's appearance. In a materialistic and affluent society the sovereignty of consumption fuels the very dissatisfactions that possessions are supposed to still. The practice of medicine in such a society is not immune to the consumerist ethic and, often, that means medicine is deeply influenced by market demands rather than therapeutic needs (see MacIntyre 1975; Schacht and Pemberton 1985).

In various ways, the idea of character being immanent in appearance has endured into the modern era as part of an authenticating narrative that establishes the self as centrally important. The value of appearance, and the sanctions attached to an unconventional appearance, are enunciated daily through the authenticating narratives of the time. The value of appearance is accepted as an axiom of social life, in bold disregard of the literary roots of this idea in the supernatural, and its historical legacy in a myriad of pseudo-sciences such as physiognomy, phrenology, augury, astrology and chiromancy. It may appear incongruous that in our society of technological sophistication, where it seems that the mysteries of nature, the human body and mind are being constantly unravelled, that we retain a strong belief in the value of physical appearances as an accurate reflection of individual character. Nonetheless, it would seem that a hegemony of appearance is still in effect. Our appearance and performance create an impression of a particular character. The fashioning of appearance becomes the means for representing ourselves as being in possession of certain characteristics. Modern medicine has played an important part in promulgating these ideas through its proclaimed ability to reshape and perfect the human body, irrespective of whether the body is fully functional or not. Through these promises to sculpt appearance, modern medicine has inadvertently underscored the physiognomic claim that appearance is important, not only in the revelation of individual character but also in the maintenance of modern social life.

The current appetite for alterations to the human form is not a reflection of any increased physical deterioration that leaves most of us in need of medicine's sophisticated services to restore and reshape us. Rather, it is more the case that the proliferation of consumer goods and services, which have developed in this era of competitive sociality, are expanding under the influences of the prevailing modern narrative that establishes the self-centred self. In these unexplicated social directives, the immanence of character in physical appearance is again being pronounced. The axiom is that one can shape one's appearance as one would like to be. This, then, is the era of self-production, as is vividly seen in the next chapter on the face lift.

Part II
Signs of the Modern Self

3

The Face Lift

A desire for cosmetic surgery has until recently been associated with psychological disturbance. Jacobson *et al.* (1960) found that males seeking cosmetic correctives had serious emotional problems. MacGregor (1967) agreed that the importance of psychological disturbance could not be overlooked, but she also recognized that some cosmetic procedures were procured as a result of social expectations. She found that the reading of character from outstanding facial features such as a receding chin, hooked nose, malformed ears and visible scars regularly disadvantaged their owner; such individuals were attributed with unappealing traits. In instances where the individual's life chances were being jeopardized by appearance, MacGregor recommended that corrective surgery be employed. Embedded in this view are elements of physiognomic reasoning, in particular, that facial features are tacitly employed to reveal human character. MacGregor also found that the more minor the physical defect, the greater were the individual's expectations that its surgical correction would substantially transform his or her life (MacGregor 1973:27).

MacGregor's observations indicate prevailing views on the ideal attributes of the human body. Her observations record that we are increasingly prepared to tamper with our features as a means of altering appearance in order to approximate more

81

closely a cultural ideal. Furthermore, the inflated expectations attached to surgical corrections of minor defects strongly suggest that there may be a perennial lack of fit between our desired and actual appearance. Indeed, the availability of surgical and other techniques for altering appearance may produce a chronic sense of discontent with our appearance. These changes in how we see ourselves and, more specifically, an increasingly commonplace discontent with our physical appearance, make the body seem as if it were a commodity and, like other commodities, susceptible to the hyperbole of a consumer ethos which represents the continual change and upgrading of goods as being a most desirable way of life (see MacIntyre 1975; Linden 1979; Haug 1986).

It follows from the increasing commodification of the body that the surgical reshaping of the face and body has become more generally acceptable and no longer thought to be indicative of psychological disturbance (Spira *et al.* 1974; Baker and Gordon 1980). There are now several commonly available procedures by which appearances can be significantly altered, for example, blepharoplasty in which the eyelids are reconstructed, rhytidectomy or face lift, rhinoplasty in which the nose is re-profiled and mammaplasty in which breast size is either reduced or augmented. Other techniques such as hair transplantation, chemabrasion and dermabrasion are also available, as are abdominal lipectomy (Grazer *et al.* 1980), buttock reduction (Lewis 1980), otoplasty or correction of the ears (Kryslova and Fahoun 1988), penile prostheses (Nellans *et al.* 1976), the surgical removal of underarm sweat glands, which has been especially popular amongst young women (Bretteville-Jensen *et al.* 1975; Eiseman 1975), the surgical creation of dimples in the cheeks or the midpoint of the chin by cicatricial adhesions (Rees and Wood-Smith 1973:510–11), and corrective jaw surgery including mentoplasty, which is the reshaping of the chin, often by silicone implantation. Some procedures are performed in conjunction with others, so, for example, Grazer *et al.* (1980:749) have suggested that abdominoplasty can be simultaneously undertaken while a face lift, hysterectomy or tubal ligation is being performed.

Numerous surgical procedures have developed in response to

fashions in physical appearance. Little toe ectomies were popular when women were wearing pointed and high stiletto-heeled shoes (Lakoff and Scherr 1984:179). In recent years, urbanized and consumer-oriented Japanese and Korean women have made blepharoplasty or eyelid surgery much more common (Rinaldo 1986); indeed, an estimated fifteen thousand surgeries are performed annually in Japan's three hundred or more private clinics. The cost of the surgery is equivalent to a professional woman's salary for three months. Often in the Japanese and Korean hospitals where these cosmetic procedures are undertaken, clothes boutiques and other cosmetic departments are also present; dental modification is, for example, popular. Rinaldo (1986) noted that the Japanese medical profession has developed sophisticated cosmetic techniques, largely as a result of the demand to repair a population with extensive radiation burns following the bombings of Hiroshima and Nagasaki. Elsewhere, other cosmetic fashions prevail; for example, in America, extensive dental procedures, which provide straighter, larger, whiter teeth, and hip-shaving, which reduces the width of the hip bones and gives women a slimmer silhouette, are popular. Overall, throughout the Westernized world, the menu of cosmetic procedures has steadily expanded in recent years.

The documentary film, Daisy: The Story of a Face Lift, by Michael Rubbo (1983), is an accessible study of popular attitudes toward reconstructive surgery. The film records a two-month period in the life of Daisy de Bellefeuille, before and after a face lift. Daisy held an executive position with the National Film Board of Canada. She had been married and divorced three times, her age was indeterminate although her children were adult. She was, by any account, an attractive woman, well-dressed, affluent, with a successful career. When the film was shown on American television in the weekly magazine programme, Frontline (1983), the host Jessica Savitch opened with the remark, 'It is believed there were somewhere around four hundred thousand cosmetic surgeries performed this year in North America.' An exact number is hard to ascertain because the procedure is elective, and often performed in day clinics, private hospitals, surgeons' rooms and so on, where the data collection is difficult to arrange and often unreliable. Savitch went on to describe how the importance of beauty in modern society has become ambiguous. While most mass media advertisements glorify physical beauty and present myriad examples of people's lives being radically transformed because of a change in their physical attributes, people are also instructed that 'it's what's inside that counts.' Savitch then referred to attitude polls which regularly showed that physical beauty was regarded as less important than other, more abstract qualities such as good reputation, industriousness and the ability to gain financial wealth. Savitch wryly interpreted the mixed messages of these bits of information as advocating that we should make every effort to stay as youthful and beautiful as possible, and use any means available to do so, but that we should not admit to this preoccupation because the value of the person is supposed to rest with other attributes, and not his or her physical appearance.

Against this background of a high cultural premium placed on physical appearance, the reasons Daisy could summon up to explain her desire for a face lift were predictably amorphous. She could enumerate various reasons, but there were no considerations more important than any other. By the same token, none of her reasons seemed fully explanatory. Initially, she suggested that it was men's greater appreciation of attractive women that had convinced her to get a face lift. In the film, she asked her friend Dave, 'Are looks important to men, or aren't they?' When he answered in the affirmative, she asked further, whether it was first impressions which were important to men; 'Before you open the package, you look at the wrapping?' and again, Dave answered in the affirmative. Sheila, Dave's wife, interjected with the common denial, 'I thought it was personality which was the most important and not the wrapper!' but, again, Dave gave emphasis to appearance with his comment, 'A man, I think, is attracted to the nicer package.'

Daisy had accepted that the way she appeared to men was more important than, in turn, their appearance for her. She seemed resigned to this double standard as a natural feature of life. For herself, she judged a man by what he said and not on his physical appearance: 'No man's ever attracted me until he's opened his mouth and said something.' However, she had accepted that her own personal appearance and grooming were vitally important to men and had worked hard all her life to ensure she was always at her most attractive. It was because of this lifelong concentration on physical appearance that Daisy saw her face lift as necessary. As she explained, 'If I look better, if I feel better, life will probably treat me better. And if I find a man, fine. But it's not for that that I will do it or that I expect it.' On another occasion, Daisy stated that she wanted the face lift 'to stave off whatever horrid future one has to face'. For Daisy, ageing was a problem. She found herself confused over what was appropriate behaviour now that she could no longer confidently claim for herself a sexual self-image: 'If I start to look at a man the way I used to look at them, sort of faintly flirtatious, because I'm incredibly romantic, do I make a total ass of myself?' Having the face lift meant she could restore herself as a sexual object and, in so doing, would know better how to conduct herself.

In order that the face lift was not seen as the prerogative of 'vain women', Rubbo included a man's face lift in the film. Peter was middle-aged and physically large, but having recently lost 120 pounds in weight, felt self-conscious about the loose skin below his chin. He wanted a face lift to improve his appearance. Even though Peter's story was included in Rubbo's film, it would be misleading to generalize that men are as willing as women to endure the discomforts of surgery in order to improve and preserve their appearance. Although appearance is regarded as important to both sexes, and there are various market indicators which suggest that men are taking their grooming more seriously, that they are buying more cosmetics and seeking beauty treatments, nonetheless, it is women who more commonly resort to surgery.

Rubbo included in the film various interviews with experts who reinforced the idea that the management of appearance was increasingly important in modern life. Rubbo showed these experts reporting on how valuable physical appearance and style could be in the job interview. For example, one expert in personnel consultancy claimed that employers made up their mind to employ a candidate within the first four minutes of the face-to-face encounter. When the job interview

85

was for more prestigious positions, say, an executive position at the highest echelons in the organization, the decision-making process was reduced to about twenty seconds. Rubbo's expert personnel consultant claimed emphatically that appearance was all that mattered. In the executive job interview, it could be safely assumed that the individual was well qualified for the position – reaching the interview stage was assurance enough of that. Hence, the actual interview was relatively empty of content and the emphasis was covertly on the physical appearance and demeanour of the candidate. The personnel consultant's conclusion was that 'this is a disturbing idea' because 'it's not the way we feel that things ought to be.'

Rubbo interviewed another expert, psychologist Michael Kalick from the University of Massachusetts, about the importance of appearance. Kalick suggested that better-looking criminal defendants had a better chance of a more lenient sentence, and nicer-looking schoolchildren were considered brighter by their teachers. This is the halo effect which numerous psychological researchers have documented. Kalick referred to his own experiments on the impressions people made on others before and after they had cosmetic surgery. In an experimental situation, he showed photographs of individuals before and after surgery. Those who saw photographs of the post-operative individuals attributed to them more highly valued and desirable personal traits such as being 'kinder, warmer, more sociable'. Those who saw photographs of individuals untouched by surgery were less impressed by them, describing them in less definite terms. Kalick's conclusions were that plastic surgery made a substantial difference to the way in which individuals were perceived by others. The better-looking person was repeatedly attributed with other valued human qualities; furthermore, this attribution improved their social performance. Kalick was subsequently drawn to the conclusion that if plastic surgery provided the individual with better life chances, then it should be more commonly used. Marwick (1988), in a historical study of personal appearance, has argued that the individual's physical beauty has always been effective in bringing about his or her social advancement. Although Marwick would not strenuously argue that physical beauty was more important in our times than in those before, he would, nonetheless, suggest that worldly successes, and the ability to be socially mobile, can be positively affected by a handsome or beautiful physical appearance. Such viewpoints are wholly complementary with physiognomic reasoning, even though physical appearance nowadays has less to do with astrological influences and the given essences of character, and more to do with the availability of techniques that can reshape and fashion the body on demand. Such preoccupations are not wholly modern; in a historical account of medicine, Pouchelle (1990) has referred to the beauty instructions of Henri de Mondeville, a fourteenth-century French physician and embalmer, who recommended depilatories such as hot needles in the hair follicles, and the use of pitch to pull out hair. It was accepted that the cultivation of a beautiful appearance often required techniques that improved on nature.

The common interpretation of the psychological data on appearance is to support the individual's desire for altering his or her shape whether it be by surgery or some other means. After all, if appearance is so important in determining life chances, and if it is by appearance that people are judged, then it would seem to be advantageous to seek cosmetic or corrective surgery. Kalick condemned the emphasis placed upon appearance because it allowed people 'to discriminate on the basis of appearance even more'. Nevertheless, as physical appearance has been repeatedly demonstrated as important in improving one's life chances, and as reconstructive surgery is a readily available means for improving appearance, then the general and professional response has been supportive of the view that transmogrifying opportunities should be used more often.

This type of medical incursion into physical appearance suggests an increasingly utilitarian attitude toward the body. It is as if the body were a utensil – a car, a refrigerator, a house – which can be continuously upgraded and modified in accord with new interests and greater resources. With the greater availability of surgical procedures and various reshaping techniques, the body does not have to be seen as a limitation on aspirations and activities but, instead, can be regarded like other commodities as a plastic instrument to be moulded to suit the individual's ambitions. In turn, this idea is compatible with there being fashions in cosmetic surgical procedures. For example, the creating of dimples and chin implants were more popular in the late 1960s and early 1970s than they are now. Chemabrasion was more popular then than it is now, although, the fashion in this procedure may be returning (Parkin 1989), and breast enlargement was popular in the 1980s whereas breast reduction was more popular in the 1970s.

The use of reconstructive procedures has been made more popular by the recent sophistication of surgical techniques. The development of better instrumentation and surgical procedures, including binocular magnifying lenses for the surgeon, better illumination in the operating theatre, the availability of air drills for cutting bone and planing skin, have meant quicker, less traumatic operations and better results (Meredith 1988:15). These various medical procedures, in conjunction with the social influences that have emphasized appearance, have helped to forge a cultural narrative or backdrop against which the human body is viewed more like a commodity which can be shaped, styled and reconstructed to approximate more closely the individual's ideal physical form. The stigma attached to cosmetic surgery, especially for men, has been greatly reduced, and although it is women who more commonly endure these procedures, there is a greater acceptance, in general, of any process which reshapes the face and body. Indeed, the increasing number of media and public figures, both male and female, who admit to having cosmetic surgery demonstrate that any residual stigma attached to these procedures is minor.

If we accept that physical attractiveness is a shared value and that most people are swayed by appearance in their judgement of others, a number of questions arise. To what lengths will an individual go to fashion the body in accord with prevailing ideals? Is it an acceptable preoccupation for the individual to spend substantial amounts of time and money on the pursuit of a particular self-image? Is the availability of an ever-increasing range of reconstructive surgical procedures a legitimate use of medical resources and professional expertise? Is the growth of industries concerned with the production and marketing of fashionable items, which, in turn, means a high turnover and high wastage of goods, an acceptable feature of a late twentieth-century economy? Is the cultivation or fashioning of physical appearance the most interesting way in which character can be expressed and conveyed to others? What are the human costs of a cultural endorsement that fashions the body by plastic and reconstructive surgery? What consequences can it have on human sociality that an increasingly popular means for meeting ideals of appearance supports, as well, an increasingly lucrative market in medical activity? In short, can the emphasis given to human appearance, as a measure of character and social value, be legitimated after exploring the nature of the techniques employed to fashion appearance and the implications they hold for social life in general?

Rhytidectomy, rhytidoplasty, meloplasty and cervicofacial meloplasty are the medical names for the surgical procedure known as the face lift. The operation has the effect of tightening the skin over the face and, thereby, smoothing out and even eliminating wrinkles. Often, the skin of the neck is included in the procedure. The individual's desire for such surgery may be to appear younger but surgeons insist the effect is that one looks better, not younger. The neotenic elements of this desire are clear; that is, the younger we appear to be, the more likely it is that we are to possess socially useful attributes. Goldwyn, a plastic surgeon, has commented that (1980:693) 'some older patients may unconsciously want literally a new lease on life – a quid pro quo, "if I look younger, I will live longer." With the realization postoperatively that such a Faustian transaction has not been and cannot be made, a few patients may become disappointed, depressed and dissatisfied.'

At one time the face lift candidate was most commonly a woman in middle age, at that period of her life which Rees and Wood-Smith (1973:19), both plastic surgeons, have patronizingly described as being 'when disappointments outweigh surprises', when children have matured and physical decline has begun. Fredricks (1974:537–43) has data in support of the conventional assumption that the use of cosmetic surgery is more widespread amongst women; of one hundred consecutive face lifts, he reported that ninety-six were women and four men. Similarly, Berry (1980:664–73) noted that in a ten-year period, of thirty-eight face lifts only one client was male, of thirty-six eyelid corrections, three were for men, and of the fourteen combined eyelid and face lift, all were women. He also reported that over 90 per cent of women underwent surgery because they wanted to 'look better', but only 9 per cent of male clients reported this as their reason. However, the clientele has changed. Now, younger women and more men are approaching the plastic surgeon (Connell 1985:152; see also Kahn and Simon 1980:678–92) because the circumstances of competitive employment have brought a new emphasis to an appearance of youthfulness and vigour.

The limitations of plastic and reconstructive surgery are repeatedly mentioned by medical practitioners and surgeons; however, even though the effects of cosmetic surgery are limited, the promised rewards of a rejuvenated appearance maintain the general enthusiasm for the procedures. The ideal recipient of cosmetic surgery, as described by plastic surgeons, is the individual who least needs it. According to Rees (1973b:136), the ideal face lift candidate is a woman in her middle forties who is thin and has a prominent or bony facial structure. As well, she should have skin that has not degenerated from the ageing process, nor has it been overly exposed to the sun. A candidate is ideal when her weight has been relatively stable for some time; this means she does not have skin which has been stressed and stretched by the increase or decrease of fatty deposits that accompany fluctuations in weight. The woman who has a more olive skin rather than a fair, thin skin, and who does not have fine 'prune wrinkles' is also an ideal candidate for a face lift. Some surgeons extend the age range for the ideal client; Goldwyn, for example, allows the ideal patient to be over sixty years, but the other recommended characteristics of olive, untanned skin and strong facial bone structure, are similar to those suggested by Rees. She should be 'of slender build, with soft, smooth skin and minimal subcutaneous fat, with a family history of youthful aging (sic), without serious illness, emotional trauma, or weight fluctuation after operation, and with the desire and skill to augment the surgical improvement by makeup, hairstyling, and enhancing clothes' (Goldwyn 1980:693). The medical definition of the ideal client with the 'soft, smooth skin' and the 'family history of youthful ageing' is probably not the person who commonly desires a face lift. As the limitations of the surgery are largely determined by the individual's skin type, healing abilities and her facility with augmentative aids like cosmetics and fashionable clothes, the results of fashioning the body only by surgery must be frequently disappointing. Nonetheless, the popularity of the face lift for women has been increasing (Meredith 1988:12).

According to the beauty editor for *Vogue* magazine, Bronwen Meredith, who recommends cosmetic surgery and most other techniques for enhancing appearance, it must be realized that there is some chance of incurring long-term damage from a face lift (1988:20–7). A face lift always involves cutting the skin and this means there will be scarring. Some scars can become hypertrophic, that is, enlarged, thick, dark in colour and disfiguring due to the formation of fibrous tumours called keloids which appear in the connective tissue of the skin. There is no preventative against hypertrophic scarring or keloids, so the risk of unsightly scarring as a result of cosmetic surgery is always present. If keloid scarring does occur, the tissue can be injected with cortico-steroids for several weeks, sometimes months, in order to blanch the scar. Whilst this treatment may reduce the high red colouring, it does little to reduce the prominence and ropiness of the scar tissue (Kahn and Simon 1980:685). There are other risks as well; for instance, there can be injury to the facial nerve which leaves numbness or reduced sensation. Parkin reported numbness in her outer cheeks some three months after the face lift, but was confident of it vanishing in time (Parkin 1989:40). In some cases, if the nerve or its branches are severed, then permanent paralysis will result. Other undesired consequences from surgery can be hair loss along the line of incision, and haematomas which are localized swellings of clotted blood.

With cosmetic surgery, an incompetent or inexperienced surgeon can dramatically exaggerate the legacies of the surgery. As with all other medical treatments, the professional expertise of practitioners must be taken by the client on faith and reputation. The client has very little knowledge about the services being sought or the level of competence of the performing surgeon. With these risks in mind, the individual electing to have a face lift or some other cosmetic procedure must have a very strong desire to alter and improve his or her appearance. Such a desire speaks eloquently of the chthonic cultural belief in the value of physical appearance.

Usually, the face lift or rhytidectomy is confined to the lower face below the eyes. An upper rhytidectomy or brow lift, which attempts to correct the horizontal wrinkles on the forehead and vertical glabellar furrows between the eyebrows, is most often performed as a separate surgical operation. The face lift or rhytidectomy is performed under a general anaesthetic and takes between one and a half to four hours. The individual is generally in hospital for several days. Kaye (1980:656) has suggested that the forehead lift can be performed using a local anaesthetic, as can otoplasty, the surgical correction of the ears; however, this depends upon the individual's tolerance for physical discomfort.

The surgical procedure of the face lift begins with lengthy incisions down the edge of the face in front of each ear. Most often, the incision extends above the ear for a further two or three inches beyond the hairline into the scalp. At the other end, the incision continues the full length of the ear, around the earlobe, following the natural curves, then the incision veers at a right angle across the bony ridge behind the ear and continues beyond the hairline into the scalp for several centimetres. The incisions carried beyond the hairline require close trimming of the hair. At the end of the surgery, these bald areas are usually not perceptible as much of this skin is removed. However, the scar tissue along the incision will not sustain hair growth and bald patches will be evident along that line. Fahoun has remarked that this baldness is always a source of client dissatisfaction and he has recommended, as a solution, the further surgical procedure of transplanting hair-bearing skin to these areas (1987:88–92).

After the first incision is made, beginning with the section in front of the ear, a process of loosening or undermining the facial skin begins, with the skin from the cheeks being lifted, exposing the soft tissue and muscles beneath. The skin peels back easily making the face appear as if it were a mask. How much skin is undermined or loosened determines the extent of the face lift. Excess skin on the neck is the easiest to correct. After the full skin flap has been loosened, the pull which constitutes the face lift is made and the skin is re-draped over the bony framework of the face. The direction of the pull, and the extent of the pull, are the essential ingredients for a good face lift.

In some face lifts, the soft tissue beneath the skin flap is also lifted. This is done by making a pleat in the flesh and sewing over the length of the tuck. Following surgery, the ridge of flesh can be felt under the skin; it may even be visible but it will eventually subside. This procedure is employed when the face is very full, and when the pull of the external skin flap may not be strong enough to hold or smooth over the deposits of fatty tissue beneath the skin (Rees 1973b:170; Connell 1985:137). To increase the success of the face lift, fat removal or subcutaneous sculpturing lipectomy is becoming more common (Connell 1985; Parkin 1989).

Often the face lift is recommended as a two-stage operation. The first surgical operation can be greatly enhanced if it is followed by a further operation about eighteen months later. The second or encore surgery has the effect of tightening whatever skin may have relaxed after the first procedure and then the face lift will remain relatively stable for a further five to seven years (Hirshowitz 1978). Rees has recommended that the individual have the first face lift in the early to mid-forties, the second in the fifties, the third in the sixties and so on, remembering that the fair-skinned woman will require multiple surgeries at closer time intervals than will the olive-skinned woman (1973b:139; Connell 1985:152–6).

After the face lift surgery, the face and ears are bound with pressure bandages. They are removed after two days, at the same time as the stitches, but for the next six weeks or so the face will show extensive signs of bruising and swelling. Eventually, these subside and the results of the face lift become visible. During the recovery period, pain and discomfort are

felt, particularly around the ears where the majority of incisions and stitching occurred. Rees and Wood-Smith (1973:22)
have recommended to their fellow surgeons the very great need
to warn their patients that 'there is a temporary period of slight
emotional depression immediately following surgery, during
the period when you (the patient will) look your worst.'

The effect of a face lift is to realign the shape of the face.
With men, this can create awkward moments. The stretching of
the face means that the boundaries of the beard are extended.
Where the skin has been pulled back from under the chin and
jaw and sewn into the hairline at the back of the ears, there will
be bearded skin, and shaving in this awkward area behind the
ears will be necessary. When the surgical procedure has been an
upper rhytidectomy or brow lift, which includes the smoothing
out of wrinkles along the forehead and the vertical furrows
between the eyes, the risk is that the hairline will be significantly disturbed. The procedure can be performed with an incision
in the eyebrows; this can disturb the hair growth and sometimes produce asymmetry in the eyebrows, resulting in a distorted appearance. Another procedure for the brow lift is to
make the incision across the dome of the head, virtually from
the tip of each ear. The skin is then rolled back as if inverting a
rubber ball and the fascial fibres are severed from the under-
surface of the skin allowing the brow to be pulled further back
over the dome of the head. To eliminate the vertical furrows
between the eyes, the corrugator muscles which lie under the
eyebrow close to the nose are cut, and the vertical muscle tissue
between the eyes needs to be crushed. This will diminish the
action of this tissue and allow for the smoothing out of any
vertical folds (Castanares 1980:644–51). Another treatment for
the furrows between the eyebrows is the injection of silicone to
fill out the corrugation (Rees 1973b:174). The use of silicone,
however, has been continuously problematic. It is prone to
migrate through the body, forming cysts and tumours, causing
damage to other healthy tissues and inducing liver disease,
including hepatitis (Ellenbogen *et al.* 1975; Lakoff and Scherr
1984:173). In the process of filling in deep furrows, only micro
amounts of silicone can be introduced at any one time. Fibrous
tissue must be encouraged to grow over the foreign silicone

drop thereby holding it in place, and this must occur before another injection of silicone can be given. Filling out a wrinkle may take ten or more injections interrupted by lengthy time periods between each treatment (Meredith 1988:41).

The major difficulty with the brow lift is the extensive incision across the head. Peeling the skin from the forehead can result in extensive damage to the natural hairline which, in turn, may induce hair loss (Rees 1973b). As well, this procedure has the effect of significantly lifting the eyebrows and changing their line of growth so that the facial appearance of the individual is markedly altered, sometimes giving a look of perpetual surprise. Because the wrinkles along the forehead and between the eyes are most often produced by muscular tension it is not sufficient to stretch the external skin in order to smooth them out. The muscular tension will continue and the wrinkles will recur. The best result is obtained when the muscle tissues are severed, but this can have the result of diminished sensation, even total numbness. Another area of relatively unsuccessful correction is the deep line of the nasolabial crease, the so-called laugh-line that extends from the edge of the nose to the corners of the mouth. These, as well as the parallel wrinkles along the forehead and the deep glabellar frown between the brows, are the hardest to correct.

Blepharoplasty is a reconstructive procedure which predates the face lift. Well before the practice became popular in the West, blepharoplasty was a procedure favoured by Orientals who sought the construction of a superior palpebral fold (Boo-Chai 1963). Blepharoplasty is the surgical shaping of the eyelids. It has always been a delicate procedure because its effect on the symmetry and general expression of the face is marked. The sagging of the upper eyelid is characteristic of ageing, and while it is not thought to interfere with eyesight, many claim to have their sight improved when the lid is reduced (Rees 1973a:46). Blepharoplasty can correct puffy eyes and the look of dissipation associated with them. The procedure involves the excision of skin and the removal of fatty tissue from both the upper and lower eyelids. It can be a dangerous procedure in that there is little room for mistakes in this area of the face (Fahoun 1988:10–13). When too much skin is removed from the eyelids, they will not close properly and this endangers the cornea. Rees has suggested that the repair of the eyelids is the most demanding procedure for the surgeon; not only are limitations imposed by the thin skin in this area of the face but also the eyes have great significance in our physiognomic reading of character. That is, if the procedure has a poor result and an unnatural appearance occurs, then there are far-reaching consequences because 'the eyes project sorrow, happiness, elation – the gamut of human emotions' (Rees 1973a:46).

Much the same could be suggested for other popular cosmetic procedures such as otoplasty, rhinoplasty, augmentation mammaplasty and abdominoplasty. Otoplasty is surgery on the ear which is undertaken most often to correct ears that are too prominent. The procedure, as with most others, is usually performed under a general anaesthetic, although a local anaesthetic can be used with adults (Kryslova and Fahoun 1988). The procedure frequently involves the removal of cartilage and the excision of skin. Post-operatively, the individual has the discomfort of wearing pressure bandages for a week or so, and sleeping with an elastic head-band covering the ears for a further four to six weeks.

Aesthetic rhinoplasty or nose correction is the most common form of facial surgery (Meredith 1988:10). It is a relatively complex procedure which relies heavily upon the expertise and judgement of the surgeon. The surgery is generally non-therapeutic and performed in response to the individual's desire to alter his or her appearance to approximate more closely a cultural ideal (Millard 1974:371). The popularity of rhinoplasty is evocative of physiognomy and it suggests a deeply held belief in its tenets. In keeping with the ancient physiognomic view that emphasized the importance of the nose, contemporary surgeons have commented that a nose correction can 'add considerably to the attractiveness and the youthful appearance' of the individual (Broadbent and Woolf 1980; Webster 1980:555). Furthermore, they pay homage to the neotenic idea that a juvenile appearance increases the social success of the individual when they state that 'a smaller nose gives the observer the unconscious impression of youth, since a child's nose is normally small and slightly retroussé'. (Webster 1980:555) Another surgeon, Millard, has pointed out that the alteration of the nose shape should be different for men and women. Men are generally taller than women, they have more people looking up at them and, subsequently, their noses are often viewed from below. It is important then that the shortening or tipping of men's noses should be less than for women. By the same token, tall women should have less taken from their noses than shorter women (Millard 1974:379).

Reshaping the nose has an unmistakable effect on the face; it changes its composition, symmetry and expression. Magli (1989:92) has reported that the ancient physiognomists identified over eighty types of noses which, in turn, indicated an equal number of moral dispositions. It would seem that surgery to alter the shape of the nose is heavily overlaid with the individual's expectations of an immediate improvement in his or her social circumstances.

Surgery on the nose is via the nostrils so there are no external scars. However, there is scarring internally which may form webbing and that, in turn, can block the air passages, causing long-term breathing problems. The surgical procedure can take several hours, there is considerable bruising around the eyes and the individual wears a face splint for a further ten days to two weeks. Rhinoplasty is an uncomfortable procedure with after-effects that endure for many months. Immediately after the surgery, a noticeable difference can be seen, but the final healing and shaping of the nose can take a further year and there may be swelling and numbness throughout this period (Millard 1974:386). The procedure does involve some risk. There can be destruction of the nose through the collapse of the bridge and septum; during surgery, when chiselling of the bone is carried out, a slight penetration of the brain can occur causing a leakage of fluid which must be repaired immediately by neurosurgery (Meredith 1988:51). As well, there are long-term effects which can be adverse. Broadbent and Woolf (1980:533) have noted that fifteen and twenty years after surgery, the skin that was undermined during the rhinoplasty may wrinkle or pucker producing a distinctly unnatural appearance along the sides of the nose. Sometimes, a widening of the nose happens or a gradual shifting to one side. After many years, where implants have been used to reshape the tip of the nose, there may be some mobility and eventual extrusion as the body's immune system works to reject the foreign material (Webster 1980:548–56).

There are now a wide range of cosmetic procedures; their availability is determined to a large extent by fashion. In recent years there has been a return to fashion of the chemabrasion. This procedure is a means for smoothing out fine facial wrinkles which the surgical procedure of the face lift does not always remedy. The chemical peel or chemabrasion can be recommended instead of or as a means of delaying a face lift. It can also be used several years after the initial face lift, again, as a means of delaying the encore rhytidectomy.

In chemabrasion, an exfoliative agent such as phenol or diethyl ether is applied to the face in a mask. The chemical penetrates below the superficial level of skin, burning it; the face goes numb, the skin turns white, then red and begins to swell. Within a few hours the skin has turned brown. A second-degree burn of the face has been induced (Meredith 1988:37–9). The individual having a chemabrasion is required to stay under close medical supervision for several days, including bed rest for the first two days. On the third day, a crust of dead skin begins to form and the swelling of the face lessens. Under this crust, the face is very red in colour. On the fourth and fifth days after the treatment, lubricating ointments and gentle washing of the face are done. It can take ten to fourteen days before the crust of dead skin is fully removed from the face, leaving an inflamed and raw look which Rees (1973b) has warned can be 'frightening'. The inflammation of the skin persists for several weeks following the procedure, the high red colour can remain for weeks even months; there can be blotchiness and it is strongly recommended that the individual keep out of the sun for at least six months. As well, there may be some limitation on the opening of the mouth because of skin tension (Spira *et al.* 1974).

The chemabrasion is painful and relatively risky. The phenol, which is applied directly to the face, is absorbed into the

3 The Face Lift

bloodstream and its effects can be unpredictable and highly toxic. The moment of contact with the skin is crucial because there is no predicting the individual's response. With the first application of phenol to the face, the individual can experience faintness, muscular weakness, convulsions, decreased respiration, constricted pupils, even coma. When the procedure begins there is generally an irregularity in the heartbeat, but Baker and Gordon (1980:639) remark that it is difficult to identify its causes: it may be from excitement, or pain, or phenol absorption.

The chemabrasion is best suited for fair-skinned people with fine wrinkles. It does not suit olive-skinned people because the skin pigmentation can be altered by the process. Neither can it be used with people who have freckles over their face and neck because often the freckles are removed in the process, however, where they still remain on the neck and hands, they become, in contrast, more obvious. The procedure of chemabrasion is commonly used for wrinkle removal on the forehead and the lips, where there is no reliable surgical treatment. However, while chemabrasion has been touted as the most effective cosmetic procedure because it is consistent and gives long-lasting effects (Spira *et al.* 1974), it has its difficulties, most notably, it is extremely painful.

Dermabrasion is a further treatment for the face. It is a surgical treatment in which the skin is planed or sandpapered using a high-powered rotating wire brush or diamond-covered drum. The procedure takes thirty to forty minutes and is performed under a general anaesthetic. Sometimes, skin-grafting is involved. The procedure, like the chemabrasion, is painful. A dressing over the face must be worn for ten days. During this period, the skin is raw and oozes a yellowish liquid; after about thirty-six hours, a scab forms which reduces the oozing. As with chemabrasion, there is extensive swelling and the skin is extremely sun sensitive for several months (Meredith 1988:36; McCoy 1977). Dermabrasion has been considered a more useful procedure than chemabrasion where there is deep scarring caused by acne or other epidermal diseases, and where there are venous blemishes.

Breast augmentation and reconstruction is the most popular

body surgery (Pickering *et al.* 1980:704; Meredith 1988:11). It takes about two hours under general anaesthetic and a hospital stay of three to four days (Meredith 1988:68). However, more recently, the popularity of the procedure has meant that many treatments are offered on an out-patient basis by entrepreneurial medical practitioners. A great deal can go wrong in this procedure but this has not adversely affected its popularity. The surgeons Pickering, Williams and Vecchione (1980:696–706) have reported on the troublesome history of the use of implants for breast augmentation. The early techniques used injections of paraffin or silicone but there were problems with the migration of the material to other parts of the body, the formation of cysts and necrosis of the skin. The grafting of dermal-fats to enlarge the breasts was also used, but they tended to be absorbed into the body fairly quickly (Watson 1980:950–5). Solid implants were then developed; initially, these were sponges of various kinds made from terylene wool, polyvinyl or polyethylene. These sponges soon hardened in situ, with an accompanying accumulation of fluid that needed to be drained from the breast. As the sponges were made from foreign materials, extrusion was a frequent occurrence. In 1963 the Dow Corning company, which is well known for its quality kitchenware, produced the silastic prosthesis. This device had a lengthy period of popularity, as did an inflatable silicone bladder developed about the same time. The rejection of these implants by the body's immune system was reduced by the administration of steroids. However, there were other problems with these devices. For instance, when the prosthesis was fixed permanently to the breast wall by an adhesive patch, the woman experienced a great deal of discomfort. The implants often became rock hard, and when there was breast ptosis or drooping, the implant remained in place as a ridge or undulation on the chest wall. This was extremely disfiguring and generally required further surgery for correction. Women with these implants reported a sense of weightiness when they were supine, and because of the hardness of the breasts, they were unable to lie comfortably in a prone position. In about thirty-five per cent of cases, implants calcify and become overgrown with fibrous tissue. When this occurs, they need to be removed

3 The Face Lift

by surgery – an often strenuous procedure because the calcified, rock-hard implants may need to be chiselled from the chest wall. During the exertions of the surgeon, further damage to nerve endings and skin can occur (Meredith 1988:68–77). Pickering *et al.* (1980:704) have also reported of the dangers to the systemic health of women after surgical breast augmentation. Notably, women with implants seem to suffer more from severe upper respiratory infections. Goldwyn (1980) has noted that the most common problems with breast surgery are a decreased sensitivity to the nipple-areola, a high risk of necrosis of skin, glands and surrounding tissue, asymmetry of the breasts and scarring from the surgical incisions.

The practice of mammaplasty or breast reconstruction began in cases where the breasts had been surgically removed, often following cancer surgery. An early method of breast reconstruction involved breast-sharing. That is, the remaining breast was split and one half was placed over the site of the mastectomy (Bostwick 1981:2). This procedure had its obvious drawbacks; it required further surgery on a breast of healthy tissue, and it risked the breast by situating it over previously diseased tissue. It is now more common after mastectomy to implant a prosthesis. The prosthesis is 'a thin-walled shell of silicone containing a treacle-like silicone gel; this gives a normal consistency on palpation' (Watts 1982:417). However, much can go wrong (Watts 1982:425) for instance, after the mammaplasty the breasts may appear to be of unequal size. In cases of bilateral implantation, one prosthesis can become distorted in shape for no apparent reason. Furthermore, the silicone can bleed into the surrounding tissue (Watts 1982:424), the implant can burst, migrate and leak, thereby endangering other body parts (Ellenbogen *et al.* 1975). These problems notwithstanding, mammaplasty is a very popular surgical procedure, not only following mastectomy, but for cosmetic reasons alone. Knorr and his associates (1968) have suggested that the popularity of the procedure is an indictment of women and their vanity; it has been Knorr's view that women who desired breast augmentation were inclined to both hysteria and depression. Watts (1982:409) has defended the procedure on the basis that women are deeply psychologically disturbed when

are damaged or undeveloped. In both instances,
ing this procedure are regarded as victims of their
ogy.

rvations omit from consideration the sociological
value placed on stereotypical appearance and, in particular,
breasts which are commonly regarded as an icon of femininity.
As well, the differential status of men and women and the
varying standards of physical attractiveness expected of them
are an important element in the purchase of these cosmetic
procedures. The comments of surgeons rarely acknowledge
these other influences. Heilbrun has commented on how rare it
is that a woman can ignore her physical appearance, and when
she does, it is frequently accompanied with stigmatizing comments on her lack of femininity and social awareness.

> The sense of conforming to the ideals of attractive womanhood
> is one that sustains many women in our culture as they grow
> older. To 'let oneself go' is to resign one's sense of oneself as a
> woman and therefore, in many ways, as a person ... Women
> are, of course, encouraged to be concerned with their physical
> attractiveness; for that reason it requires great courage to ignore
> one's appearance. (1989:54)

A recently developed surgical procedure to the body is that
of suction lipectomy which removes fatty deposits without
extensive surgery and the risk of scarring. The lipectomy suc-
tions fatty tissue from beneath the skin, along the same principles as a vacuum cleaner. About three pounds of fatty deposit
can be removed in half an hour. The procedure involves a salt
solution being injected under the skin which liquefies the fat
and allows it to be suctioned out as a yellow fluid. Alternative-
ly, dry fat tissue can also be suctioned out by tearing it away
from its fibrous connections. Both procedures allow for substantial amounts of fat to be removed, but there are some
adverse consequences which can require subsequent surgery
(Meredith 1988:78–87). For example, the suctioning process
may leave uneven ridges, puckers and folds of tissue beneath
the skin. Where there has been a substantial suctioning of fatty
tissue there is often an excess of outer skin which can hang like
an apron; this must be surgically excised. When these flaps are

trimmed off, there is the problem of long scars, of keloids developing and of stress along the line of the incision (Lewis 1980). The recovery from this surgical procedure, known as abdominoplasty, is uncomfortable and painful. Bed rest is required, and there must be flexion at the hips and knees to preserve the stitching, which means the individual is held in an unnatural position. At the same time, s/he must also begin moving in order to prevent blood clotting, although an upright position is impossible for about three to six weeks. So, after the surgery, the individual is forced to move about in a doubled-over position. The great attraction of the procedure, however, is the instantaneous effect of the mechanical removal of large amounts of excess fatty tissue. These results make the procedures very popular, despite the risks and discomfort (Grazer *et al.* 1980).

It may, in the first instance, seem incongruous to treat the natural properties of the body as if they were manipulable. However, advances in surgical procedures have encouraged a consumer ethic to influence our perceptions of the body. With this attitude, it is easy to insert the body into the marketplace and see it as a commodity like so many other manufactured objects. Plastic surgery on the human body has gained increasing acceptance and popularity. The body has become an object to be shaped at will, in accord with prevailing fashions and values. As we imagine we need new appliances, new possessions, new adventures and experiences to realize our social ambitions – and we are prepared to pay the price of them – so, our desires for a new physical image, a better appearance, a stronger sense of sex appeal, a more youthful appearance and so on, can be met by treating the human body as we would other consumer and fashionable items.

These are the ideas prevalent in the well-advertised services of Gilbert Eiseman, the director of the plastic surgery complex at Farmingdale, New York, and an enthusiast for the surgical treatment of cosmetic conditions (Eiseman 1975). Eiseman regularly advertises in the daily press and specialist publications such as *The Village Voice*. He has a phone-in service for the prospective client who can remain anonymous and listen to a tape-recorded message about the costs, procedures and specific

surgical treatments s/he is interested in, such as a nose correction, breast augmentation, tummy tuck, thigh shaping and so
on. The clinic receives approximately ten thousand enquiries
during a year and performs about six hundred operations.
Eiseman has reported that breast augmentation is his most
popular procedure with rhinoplasty being the second.

In the film of Daisy's face lift, Rubbo recorded the comments of Gilbert Eiseman and some of his satisfied clients. A
thirty-five-year-old woman reported that her fear of ageing and
losing her shapely body had induced her to have her breasts
augmented. This procedure made her 'feel good', so a few years
later, at age thirty-nine, she had a lower blepharoplasty, the
removal of some skin from below the eyes: 'I needed to know
that I was still young looking, still attractive'; 'even though
everyone says I looked about thirty-five, I knew I was thirty-
nine'. The same woman reported that in five more years she
planned to have Gilbert Eiseman 'do the rest of my face'.
Another young woman interviewed in the film was twenty-
three years old and had had her breasts augmented at the
Farmingdale clinic. 'It was' she says, 'the best thing I ever did.'
When Eiseman quipped predictably that 'now she's perfect',
the young woman responded in kind, 'I only wish.'

The various cosmetic procedures now readily available, from
the face lift which takes several hours of surgery, to the fifteen-
minute collagen replacement procedure which fattens up the
back of the hands and reduces the shrunken appearance associated with age, treat the body as if it were a plastic vehicle to be
restyled to suit the individual's wishes and meet the dictates of
fashion. Most of these treatments and procedures are available
to the individual only through the medical profession, which
means that many of the practices of modern medicine are not
performed for therapeutic reasons, but are to enhance, cosmeti-
cally, the physical appearance of the individual. The face lift,
tummy tuck, breast augmentation, hair transplant, stomach
staple, nose correction and so on are readily available to those
willing to meet the costs and discomforts of surgery. Increasingly, individuals troubled by their appearance can find a
remedy in the practices of modern medicine. Thus, individuals
with an unsatisfactory appearance, or who perceive themselves

to have such, can successfully look to the medical profession to intervene and correct any disjuncture between self-image and appearance.

As physical appearance continues to play an ever important role in social life, other industries and products are developing to provide advice, treatments and techniques for fashioning the body. The annual expenditure on cosmetics, for example, is about one per cent of all consumer expenditure on goods and services (*Cosmetics and Toiletries Report* 1985). Hair products, such as shampoos, gels, colourings, dyes and spray lacquers, constitute the largest segment of this market. Women spend more than twice as much money as men on all kinds of cosmetics and toiletries. It would seem that the fashioning of the body is a daily practice for women. Certainly, much is made of a woman's appearance in terms of the social position and prestige she can claim. It is no accident, in this regard, that it is women who figure predominantly in the extreme weight and size categories of the obese and anorexic. The cult of physical beauty is most fervently followed by women who well understand that much of their social status and opportunities for privilege will depend upon their physical looks. Brumberg (1988) is led to conclude from her study of anorexic women that exercising control over one's physical appearance, even to the extreme of self-starvation, has become for the contemporary woman as close to a coherent philosophy of self as can be found in a secular society.

Our contemporary attitudes toward physical appearance share many similarities with the physiognomic perspective. Our modern view, like that of the physiognomists, is still to deduce character from physical appearances, even though we readily re-shape the body and re-fashion our facial features to better approximate our self-perceptions and ideals. We know we have deliberately created an image of how we want to look, and we have employed techniques such as surgery, cosmetics and fashionable clothing, to bring this about. Despite such manipulations, we still make extensive use of the individual's appearance as a key to character.

Physical appearance thus remains an important summary of character for us, even though we know the association between appearance and character is murky and open to interpretation. Certainly, the injustices of reading character from appearance may be now better known, and the prejudices which arise from such stereotyping are more frequently resisted. Increased migration and tourism have taught us, repeatedly, that judging others by their physical appearance is misleading. The lessons of feminism, too, have been clear in this regard; the worth of women cannot be deduced from physical appearance. Yet, despite these influences, physical appearance remains a ready tool in the human commerce of the everyday, and vast industries rest upon its employment. In the next chapters, we review the endurance of this idea that character can be read from appearance and how the fashion industries, in particular, have exploited the idea.

4

The Necktie

Clothes are 'inseparable from the self' Hollander (1980:451) has declared in her analysis of the history of fashion, a bold claim made bolder by adding that clothing reflects the individual's sense of 'respect for the order of things' (1980:362). By this Hollander means that in the styles of clothing adopted *en masse* there is a perceptual ordering of the world, an authenticating narrative, that is taken to be commonsensical and unproblematic. The ways in which we dress and expect others to do so are defining limits on what we perceive as normal and orderly. For example, the man's business suit, which is a relatively new form of attire evolved from the nineteenth-century dandy's day wear, is now *de rigueur*. Clothing styles reveal the limits of the social order in so far as the styles in appearance that are now accepted as ordinary and natural were, a moment ago, new, startling, sometimes bizarre. As Hollander has explained:

> The most important aspect of clothing is the way it looks ...
> The way clothes look depends not on how they are designed or
> made but on how they are perceived ... People dress and
> observe other dressed people with a set of pictures in mind –
> pictures in a particular style. The style is what combines the
> clothes and the body into the accepted contemporary look not
> of chic, not of ideal perfection, but of natural reality. (1980:311)

If we accept Hollander's view that clothing is integral to a sense of order, then it is easy to see how clothing can be used as a rich vocabulary of tacit meanings which affect the interchanges between individuals. Again, the man's business suit is a good example. Few transactions within the corporate world would take place between men not attired in this uniform, and any man claiming the status of an economic, political, bureaucratic or judicial player must appear in this serious, sombre costume designed so as not to detract attention from the task at hand. Even when this masculine uniform is appropriated by women, still it retains its general meaning, that of indicating the importance of business. Uniformity in styles of dressing is an eloquent part of the minutiae of interpersonal exchange; in the case of the business suit, a foundation of shared meanings is being asserted throughout a masculinized, although not necessarily all male, corporate world. When the suit is recognized as either hand tailored, a Savile Row product, mass produced, fashionable, classical, *passé* or some other style, these distinctions become part of the vocabulary of social exchange. Clothes convey information to those skilled in reading them, and those who wear them purposefully. Clothing is a vocabulary, complete with evocative subtext.

The importance of clothing relates also to establishing physical appearance as a revealing sign of social identity. Although, in our ordinary day-to-day habits we are not accustomed to specifying the clues we have gathered in those first moments of an introduction, nor can we easily nominate which details of the other captured our attention and affected our attitude toward them, nonetheless, we are aware that clothing and physical appearance do have a significant influence on our attitudes toward and understanding of the other. As Davis has stated (1985:16): 'we know that through clothing people communicate some things about their persons ... but ... the actual symbolic content that elicits such interpretations eludes us.' With much the same idea in mind, Hollander has claimed that the details of dress are eloquent.

Clothing, however, like tone of voice and speed of utterance, conveys other kinds of moral quality – the texture and style and flavor of the self ... In a sense, beautiful clothes *are* beautiful manners ... Clothes make the man, not because they make up or invent what the man is or dress him up for show but because they actually create his conscious self. You are what you wear – and especially when class structure lacks rigidity ... When you are dressed in any particular way at all, you are revealed rather than hidden. (1980:444)

To assert that 'you are what you wear', especially in the contemporary consumer society where the traditional emblems of inherited class and power have been excised from the public domain, Hollander brings attention to how objects of clothing and fashions have become invested with intangible and abstract elements that pertain to the moral and social order, although, how this transposition is accomplished is extremely difficult to define. Unlike the physiognomists, to whom it seemed quite possible to point to a nose and confidently declare its owner to be melancholic or criminal, we find it more difficult to specify how this form of dress or that style of appearance leads us to think of an individual in a particular way. For example, there is general consensus that the business suit is the appropriate attire for those engaged in the work of commerce, government and the professions, so, when women take on these jobs, they are expected to dress after the male style. In this way, the outer garments have been taken as an expression of the individual's intention to act in the same way as others who are similarly attired. Women, wearing the business suit, are taken to be expressing a degree of seriousness that is associated with the corporate world. The assumption is that a similitude exists between the appearance of the individual and the demeanour, even personal characteristics, which s/he can be expected to possess. Thus, the more audacious claim is tacitly made that the suit of clothes is symbolic both of the individual's intentions to act in a given way and his or her private system of values and attitudes. However, beyond the immediate, at-first-glance interpretation of appearances, how we deduce the other's character, how we extricate social meanings from clothing styles and overall physical appearance, becomes a complex and unsystematic process. For example, to discern character differences between the wearer of a Savile Row business suit and a mass-produced one is to enter an exclusive social world where the esoteria of fabric, fibre, tailoring and aesthetics are hegemonic (Alvarez 1989). This is not the everyday world of first impressions and fleeting exchanges, although, it is a social world where sustained and enduring interactions employ physical appearance as a sign of the self.

To posit an equivalence between clothing and character, between the symbolic and the real, may pose grand philosophical problems to the epistemologist, but the association passes as a truism in the everyday world of ordinary sociation. Using fashion as a code of communication makes use of appearances as if they were reliable signposts to the nature of self and to the moral character of the individual. While it may seem absurd, unreliable and unjust to judge human capacities by appearance, we have already seen that the process has a long and varied history.

Hollander's work emphasizes the importance of fashion as an influence on the individual's appearance. She presents the argument that styles of clothing are 'evidence about changing assumptions and habits of actual seeing, and so of visual self-awareness' (1980:xii). Her position challenges the commonplace view that clothing and its fashions are little more than a constantly passing parade of frivolities and whims; instead, she has produced a strong argument that our consciousness of the human body and our understanding of aesthetics has been refracted through the shape we give ourselves through costumes.

> The 'natural' beauty of cloth and the 'natural' beauty of bodies have been taught to the eye by art, and the same has been the case with the natural beauty of clothes. The tight-laced waist, the periwigged head, and the neck collared in a millstone ruff, along with flattened breasts and blue-jeaned legs, have all been comfortable, beautiful, and natural in their time, more by the alchemy of visual representation than by the force of social change. (Hollander 1980:xiii)

Hollander regards clothing, costumes and fashions as the means by which individuals picture themselves and, subsequently, present themselves in accord with their own self-

110

4 The Necktie

image. Whether the individual's items of clothing are high fashion luxuries or the age-old traditional costumes of an ethnic identity, the style of clothing selected is a gesture made toward the generalized other, the public, in order to convey a particular impression. At the same time, Hollander appreciates that such a view can simplify the social processes at work and make clothing seem more like a mask or a form of disguise behind which we protect ourselves from others (1980:451–2). While this may be true, it is so only in part, as Hollander makes the further point that clothing styles are, more importantly, essential to the construction of consciousness and self-knowledge.[1]

The importance of clothing as an influence upon consciousness and self-knowledge is illustrated by the different ways in which we regard ourselves when clothed and when naked – a view well supported by Garfinkel (1956) and Goffman (1961) in their respective studies of degradation ceremonies, where an effective means of weakening the individual's morality and identity, is to strip him or her of clothes and hair. Primo Levi, in his powerful accounts of life in the concentration camp, has observed the same fracturing of character when people are stripped of garments. In the following remarks, he has suggested that the essence of humanity is preserved when clad;

> now a naked and barefoot man feels that all his nerves and tendons are severed: he is helpless prey. Clothes, even the foul clothes distributed (in the camps), even the crude clogs with wooden soles, are a tenuous but indispensable defense. Anyone who does not have them no longer perceives himself as a human being but rather as a worm: naked, slow, ignoble, prone on the ground. He knows that he can be crushed at any moment. (1989:113–14)

[1] It may be timely to note, here, that the argument of this book is not fully in accord with Hollander's position. In the final chapters, I make clear that I do not see clothing as a means of protecting the individual from others, or as a means to disguise the essential self. Indeed, the argument is that fashionability in appearance steers people away altogether from considerations about the nature of human character (see chapters 6 and 7 below).

Hollander has argued that it is only clothing that gives a specific perceptual knowledge of the body. Thus, when naked, we continue to perceive the body as if it should be clothed; for this reason, the naked body often results in feelings of vulnerability and shame, which is a conclusion that data from degradation ceremonies corroborate. With this kind of power over consciousness, clothing cannot be regarded as simply a cultural symbol with the function of continually reinforcing certain values and customs; it should also be seen as a device which contributes to the making of a particular manner of feeling and thinking (Hollander 1980:xiv). That is, clothes affect our self-image and our social relations. Hollander has given the instance where the individual's attention to clothes is so engrossing that it becomes a form of solipsism. Similarly, the fashion *habitué*, or in Simmel's language, the dude (1904), can develop such a deep personal concern over the details of dress that s/he has the capacity only of 'a shallow heart and a limited mind' (Hollander 1980:xiv). It is an idea also borne out by the example of the Regency dandy.

The dandy is an important figure in the emergence of modern fashions, particularly for men, because his appearance marked a distinctive break with the masculine aesthetic of the *ancien régime*. Moers's (1978) study of the Regency period and, in particular, the rise of the dandy, has demonstrated that the value placed upon external appearance at this time became increasingly important to the manners of exchange and the character of social life. Moers has cogently argued that a shift in sensibility took place when the age of consumerism was expanding, in the early nineteenth century, and a new balance was being struck in which the external appearance, particularly of men, was becoming a significant index of political and social interests. At the time, a man could demonstrate his thorough disinterest in the struggles for power and his distance or removal from ancestral wealth in the style of clothes and the mien he adopted. For a society in transition, where the fate of an individual could be decided because of his or her political allegiances, the individual could increase his or her social security by demonstrating a disinterest in any political questions. This was to become the signature of the Regency dandy; as

Moers has described, when the 'solid values of wealth and birth are upset, ephemera such as style and pose are called upon to justify the stratification of society' (1978:12).

In the Regency dandy, we encounter a sensibility which reflects an increased concern with the performance of social exchange and an obedience to style at the expense of developing authentic and engaging social relations. To focus so closely on one's style of appearance is to become distracted from concerns that are more morally transcendental, such as an involvement with the politics or injustices of the day; such attention to self-adornment has the effect of curtailing or closing off a social and political consciousness. In the case of the dandy, the dedication to self-presentation was a deliberate device by which to extol one's social superiority whilst, at the same time, repudiating and disdaining issues unrelated to one's personal concerns. The dandy's fascination with artifice and performance had the effect of investing objects with a greater social potency than any abstract humanistic concerns of social life.

The hours that George 'Beau' Brummell (1778–1840) spent on the fashioning of his appearance, and, in particular, in the preparation of his linen shirt and cravat, were essential to the claims he wanted to make for an elevated social status. In the figure of the dandy, the forerunner of the modern business suit and the necktie began their contemporary career. Brummell made neckwear famous through the singular fame of his own cravat. This article of clothing, like his trousers and coats, was plain and precise. Brummell used starched neckcloths of linen and changed them often to ensure their continual freshness. Unlike his contemporaries, Brummell rejected the fashions of the day, he declined the strong colours of embroidered cloth and turned attention away from the extravagant trimmings found on waistcoats, shoes and such like. Instead, he concentrated on the body and used his clothing to bring attention to and enhance the human frame. Thus it was that his social identity was fashioned from appearance; it was not extracted from aristocratic, occupational or political inheritances. Indeed, his heritage was minor and his income meagre but this did not prevent him claiming a vaunted social prominence. He was the newly made and self-made man and his necktie, in many ways, encapsulated that image.

Brummell was a product of the tailor and his own self-image. As such, he has provided a convenient date upon which to hang a wider social change, namely, the dawn of the self-styled, fashioned individual who was concerned with self-promotion, and who employed clothing and various items of fashion and conspicuous consumption to celebrate this new status. Banner (1983) has described much the same phenomenon in the American society of the early nineteenth century, where fashionability became increasingly common as a means of self-promotion; 'for upwardly mobile young men how they looked was important, not only as a means of business advance, but also as a measure of self-esteem' (Banner 1983:233; see also de Marly 1985).

It is fitting that the aspect of dress most cultivated by Brummell to summarize his identity claims was that decorative item, the necktie. His necktie became a pedestal for the self. It was an item of conspicuous style which was decorative, self-referencing and without function. By the delicacy of the necktie's appearance, the necessity to renew it constantly to retain its freshness and the prominence with which it was displayed on his chest, Brummell could declare his primary interests were in his own elegance and sense of aesthetics. Brummell was not purposeful or civic-minded; he was a harbinger of the new ethic, in which personal identity and character were fashioned. With Brummell's social ascendency, character no longer needed to be viewed as inherent, or even the result of ennobling moral gestures and acts. In the figure of Beau Brummell, there was the declaration of the self-produced modern individual, whose identity was fashioned from material possessions.

The use of clothing and bodily adornment as a sign of social position has a long history. The wearing of exclusive garments and insignia such as furs, silks, swords, gold chains and so on has, in the past, been an advertisement for an individual's status. The sumptuary laws of European society, between the thirteenth and seventeenth centuries, were attempts to regulate these displays and ensure the stability of the social and economic order (von Boehn 1932; Braunstein 1988:575–80). However, with industrialization of the nineteenth century and the mass production of goods, such regulation over the dispersal of goods and commodities was immediately redundant. With a plentiful supply of material goods, the individual's right to possessions, be they gold adornments, furs, silk clothes or heeled shoes, took on a different meaning. Now, the ownership and display of goods became evidence of an individual's accomplishments and attributes. Ownership made an individual appear wealthy, socially mobile, in possession of refined sensibilities and tastes. Thus, items of property took on a symbolic and representational quality; they were no longer declarations of the inherited stratification of the pre-industrial and pre-urban society, instead, they now suggested the possession of interior personal attributes.

The intensification of interest in personal appearance and clothing styles that Brummell's self-dedication exemplified remains a feature of modern social life. As Hollander has well argued, styles of clothing have become part of our perceptual horizon; they mark out the boundaries of the acceptable. When we encounter others dressed in styles of their choice, we readily conclude that we are seeing their self-representations. We have come to regard clothing and appearance as signs of the self; from outward appearance, we are prepared to deduce, sometimes accurately sometimes not, the other's claims for status, prestige, standard of respectibility, and even his or her proclivities and talents.

Sennett's (1976) analysis of eighteenth- and nineteenth-century styles of public life has provided a further example of how a reliance upon appearances distinguishes the contemporary reading of character. The effect of clothing in the mannerisms of social exchange has been to announce which rules of conduct are salient before the more demanding moment of face-to-face discourse takes place. Thus, one knows from appearance, whether one is addressing a male or female, someone of higher or lower social status, an adherent to the status quo or a deviant from it, and the manner of discourse which follows reflects these observations. Sennett draws his conclusions from the social dislocation brought about through the economic and demographic consequences of industrialism and urbanism.

The age of consumption has thoroughly transformed the individual's relationship with the material world. As Veblen also pointed out (1899:29), 'the possession of wealth, which was at the outset valued simply as evidence of efficiency, becomes, in popular apprehension, itself a meritorious act. Wealth is now itself intrinsically honourable and confers honour on its possessor.' By employing conspicuous consumption as the means to gain prestige and status, the individual has become committed to the constant purchase and updating of material goods as soon as they are available in the marketplace. This is the practice Veblen termed 'pecuniary emulation', and it rests upon the belief that in the ownership of valued goods there is a reflection of more abstract estimations about the individual's character and social value. The individual with more valued goods must be intrinsically richer and of greater worth to the society; so, the more wealth one can display, that is, the more conspicuously one can consume, the greater will be the status others will confer upon him or her. Furthermore, the more money spent on goods without any immediate utility, that is, the more luxuries and superfluities that one could own, the more prestige one can command.

For Veblen, pecuniary emulation was an indication of a society's moral bankruptcy. While he accepted that any social group would be divided by differences in levels of wealth, he did not think it inevitable or necessary that the moral assessments of social members should be calculated on that basis. For Veblen it seemed ideally possible to keep wealth as a reflection only of the individual's efficiency, without taking the next reprehensible step and making it a measure of the individual's social and moral worth. When the social group transposed wealth into a measure of moral value, then it began its moral decline. In early American capitalism, Veblen already saw that wealth was becoming a moral sign, that it was becoming an index of the individual's social worth.

In a society dominated by a consumer ethic, the mannerisms of human sociality are transformed into a form of exhibitionism where individuals in interaction are largely concerned with an exchange of status symbols and little else. Veblen maintained that in the nascent capitalism of the nineteenth century,

116

the ever-increasing variety of material objects available for purchase, and their continually fluctuating value and status, altered human sociality in so far as definitions of self-identity shifted from abstract considerations of individual sensibility, capability and morality toward the ownership of goods as sources of power, influence and prestige. Thus, social relations became an exercise in controlling the opinion of others, winning their approval, or at least, impressing them sufficiently to garner respect. In such an ethos, owning more, commanding greater reserves of wealth, translated into being a more socially valuable person.

Capitalism requires of the individual a continual desire to purchase new products. However, in order to support widespread consumption, there must be widespread wealth and, if not wealth, then credit.[2] A consumer economy needs credit to be available to the majority. It cannot be a tacit exchange of noblesse oblige and honour between the aristocrat and artisan, nor a practice restricted to a privileged few (McKendrick *et al.* 1982). With credit, the individual can display wealth through conspicuous consumption, without actually being in possession of wealth. Credit creates the opportunity to display what is not owned, but what is borrowed, feigned, self-styled or imitated. Credit is the ultimate pretence. The significance of this is that individuals can now claim social position by convincing, even

---

[2]   Prior to the twentieth century, the provision of credit was often a complex and tacit exchange of noblesse oblige and honour between the aristocrat and artisan. It was a transaction which did not always include monetary payment for goods (McKendrick *et al.* 1982). It was often deemed sufficient recompense that the purveyor of the goods, the artisan or merchant, received for his or her services the honour of being selected by an aristocratic patron. In this century, where the status differentials of feudalism have largely withered away, such a barter system holds even less appeal than it probably did for the medieval trader. The invention of credit now allows items to be purchased without the purveyor requiring much knowledge of the purchaser's resources. Modern, legal credit systems have provided protection of the purveyor from lack of payment, whilst allowing the purchaser to own goods without the financial means to do so. The act of purchase no longer depends upon the temperament or disposition of the purveyor to meet the purchaser's desire; the modern invention of credit has introduced on impersonality into the transaction which means that the only restraints upon the individual are those of a remote legal system policed by government institutions.

duping others about their wealth, superior tastes, fashionability or whatever else constitutes the social currency. In other words, it is by staging a performance, 'impression management', gossip, display, ostentation and so on, that an individual can assert a particular character and social position.

By creating the ability to live beyond one's means, by pretending to be financially stronger than one is, the age of consumerism has engendered an emphasis on the spectacular and exhibitionist. The department store has played a major part in the promulgation of this ethos. The department store was a nineteenth-century innovation. Unlike other retail outlets of the time, it was physically large, with a plethora of independent sections and various displays of goods. The proportions of the department store were capitalized upon in so far as they were designed to disorient shoppers, to induce them to lose their bearings, even to lose a sense of reality, and in this way succumb to the calculated displays of luxuries arranged on the shop floor (Miller 1981; Chaney 1983). The nineteenth-century department store was an emporium of desires (Zola 1883). Unlike the small specialist shop, or the tailor's workroom where items had to be requested, the department store enticingly displayed all its goods. As well, the price of each item was visible and fixed, and this freed the shopper from haggling with the shopkeeper at the point of purchase. In the more impersonal atmosphere of the department store, the shopper could remain anonymous and seemed, thereby, more inclined to purchase because s/he was less intimidated.

The emergence of the department store was important to the development of the consumer society because it allowed shoppers to come into closer contact than ever before with an array of alluring goods on display. As individuals walked about the store, they could stop at fashionable items and handle the goods, bringing them as it were within their grasp, imagining themselves the happy owners. The department store taught shoppers to enjoy the pursuit of that indomitable quarry, the new and fashionable. In the late twentieth century, the suburban shopping complex, with its multitude of separate shops and businesses is designed for the same effect: to provide the shopper with a safe universe in which to wander without much

118

direction, but with a topography designed to induce a sense of disorientation that makes him or her more vulnerable, but without a sense of menace, to the beckoning array of desirable goods.

The consumer ethic, the innovation of the department store, fashionability and widespread credit have heralded an era of the representational and exhibitionist. In such an age, the authenticating narrative portrays the human experiences of desire and pleasure as attached to material objects which can be possessed, purchased and traded. The body has become a vehicle for displaying valued goods, and physical appearance, shape, size, prowess and so on are read by others as if they were signs of character. Where an emphasis on appearance, performance and display develops, then the individual becomes known to the other only through image and reputation. How well one can convince others of one's claims, how well one can display oneself and control the impressions and opinions that others will form, becomes a foundation of modern sociality. Decisions to own this and not that, to desire one commodity and not another, to value these goods and disparage others, have their arbitrariness and inherent morality disguised by the banality, the commonplace nature of continuous procurement. In this way, human sociality becomes a trade in fashionable items; it is emptied of its spontaneity and easy companionship to become dominated instead by the necessity to display material goods, control impressions and cultivate reputation.

The origins of the fashioned self lie in pecuniary emulation, the invention of financial credit and the escalation of fashionability. These influences entrench in our consciousness the legitimacy of the pursuit of the new, making it seem as if the self must be continuously fashioned and re-fashioned. New products are constantly being presented, and the renewable desire for these objects, and more, affects the nature of sociality. The twinges of envy felt over the possessions of others, the prod of desire which directs the individual to shop and purchase, the anxiety that must be controlled when one believes one's possessions inadequate, the discomfort sensed when an extravagance has been purchased, are the kinds of emotions and sensations which may not appeal as particularly noble, yet,

119

these emotions are now an ordinary feature of everyday social life.

The mass manufacture and marketing of fashionable commodities, and the redefinition of these commodities as symbolic of personal attributes and achievements are key features of modern capitalism. The zenith of the consumer ethic is reached when material commodities become representative of cultural ideals. At this point, any idea or abstraction can be translated into a material object and a procurable desire. That decorative item of clothing, the necktie, well illustrates how the complex and abstract personal attributes of mood, sexuality, ambition, taste and so on have been embedded in a procurable item of fashion. In the ever-changing style of the necktie there can be buried a multitude of social messages. As an article of clothing the necktie may have negligible utility, but it remains a steadfast icon of status as well as gender.

The symbolic content of the necktie seems enriched by its ostensible lack of function. It is unarguably decorative, being worn largely as a sign both of the individual's sense of aesthetics and claims of social propriety. It remains an item of clothing that requires a degree of skilled tailoring and costly human labour in its manufacture and so, at its best, it is a relatively expensive item of clothing that allows the wearer to demonstrate a degree of idiosyncratic personal style. The necktie loses value when it is poorly made, if it hangs too long or not long enough, or if it is worn inappropriately, say, while engaging in active or dirty work. The necktie is a sign of conspicuous immobility because it is shown to its best effect when the wearer is inactive, idle, even motionless. It is a fragile and unreliable accessory in so far as it can betray one's aspirations as effectively as it publicizes them, yet, it is an accessory weighted down by the importance of first impressions; as Fraser has commented, the tie is used to transmit 'minor social messages' (1981:232). To apply Hollander's thesis to an analysis of the necktie is to see definitions of masculinity and male identity through that item of clothing. In the industrialized world where a man's social identity is submerged in the business suit or the uniform work clothes, the necktie can be made into a talisman of individuality and imbued with an exorbitant burden of identity claims.

Currently, men wear ties as part of their customary apparel; in contrast, women occasionally wear them, such as when fashion dictates. The tie varies in appearance, its size, texture, colour and shape reflect trends in fashions as well as personal preferences. Sometimes the tie is snake-thin and made of leather, or abundant, floral and cut from soft silk. Much has been made of the necktie as a flag or signpost to the wearer's mood, intentions and character. The necktie can be an emblem of social attachment, say, to a school or private club; as well, it can advertise its designer origins with references within its pattern to the well-known logos of, say, Cardin and Givenchy. This trend can be contrasted with the designer labels of most quality garments which remain inside. Some ties are more eloquent than others. Generally, the paler the tie, the more important the social occasion where it is worn, the white bowtie being the most formal. The pale tie is shown to full advantage when it is immaculately clean, unblemished. In this pristine state, it proves the adroitness of the wearer; after all, he must have refined table manners and social skills because no drip nor morsel of food has stained it. Other ties signify various meanings; the bold red tie, commonly seen against the dark suit, is purportedly eloquent of a man's sexual energy, and the American black string-tie, held by an ornamental torquoise clasp, is used to identify regional origin and to gather to its wearer the characteristics associated with the cowboy who tamed the wild west and foreshadowed American world hegemony (see Lurie 1983). The bowtie draws attention to the head and lower part of the face, it especially highlights the mouth, which is supposedly the organ through which intelligence is demonstrated. Thus, the bowtie is thought to be favoured by those men who have elected the importance of the mind over the body.

The conventional long tie runs from the prominent male larynx, along the torso and terminates as a signal to the male sex organ, particularly when the man is seated. In this capacity, the tie links together the physical symbols of virility, and as such, can be used as a psychoanalytic proboscis that demarcates a line from manhood to manliness. Freud (1927:147–58) confidently described the necktie, in an essay on fetishism, as a strong symbol of the phallus. Flügel (1930:26) continued the association by asserting all clothes aroused sexual interest and some, in particular, were signposts to the sex organs; 'clothing originated largely through the desire to enhance the sexual attractiveness of the wearer and to draw attention to the genital organs of the body.'

The modern meaning of the necktie is not all that remote from its nineteenth-century version in that it is still worn as an icon of identity and as a declaration of conspicuous consumption. The garment is also regarded as an eloquent sign of character. It may succeed in carrying out the intentions of the wearer, but just as often, it can also work against those interests. As the costume historian Quentin Bell has pointed out, wearing the wrong tie is worse than wearing none at all (1976:19). Hence, physical appearances are thought capable of transmitting opposing messages, that is, they can inadvertently reveal character against the wishes of the individual, and at the same time, successfully promote an image of character desired by the individual.

The origins of the necktie are part of a more general history of neckwear and it is difficult to specify exactly the moment when the tie appeared. It may, for instance, be an adaptation of a cravat which Croatian soldiers brought into military attire when they were enlisted in the service of the French crown in 1636 (von Boehn 1932: vol. 3, 144; Payne 1965:350). Or, the tie may have its origins with the French *crabbat* which came into fashion in 1656. Alternately, the tie may be an extension of those looped trimmings which were attached to men's outer garments, common in 1650–60, and which were known as *petite-oie* because of their resemblance to the giblets of a goose (von Boehn 142). Or, the modern necktie may be a descendent of the *steinkerk*, a new style cravat that appeared in 1692 to commemorate a French battle victory. The story goes that the French army was attacked by surprise by the forces of William III near the village of Steinkerque. The French officers had no time to arrange their cravats with usual elegance, so they flung them around their necks and slipped the ends into a buttonhole of the outer jacket. Boucher (1967:435) has described how this fashion was spread by the efforts of Mademoiselle de Rochois, a singer at the Paris Opera, who appeared wearing a lace cravat thrown nonchalantly over her coat, like the officers surprised by the enemy. As the battle had been a French victory, the fashion immediately spread throughout Paris and both men and women were seen to wear a cravat in this style.[3]

An earlier version of the necktie may have derived from the Spanish ruff common in the late sixteenth century. This ruff was a large circle of stiff linen which effectively divided the head from the rest of the body. It was a difficult garment to wear, particularly when eating and drinking because it required that the individual stretch out his or her arms in order to get around it. Nonetheless, it was popular with both men and women. By the 1630s the stiff ruff had softened into a circle of linen which lay upon the shoulders, and from there the garment may have evolved into a smaller, more simple winged collar resembling the modern Eton collar.

The history of the necktie is not precise. The tie has appeared in various guises, sometimes as a ruffle, looping trim, cravat, linen collar or bowtie. Universally, it has lacked an obvious function apart from its decorative value. Nonetheless, it has commonly been an item of luxury in human apparel and an adornment or symbol of status and fashionability. To accept that the longevity of the necktie, in its various forms, has more to do with fashionability than with utility (which is the conclusion to which the history of costume leads) is to acknowledge that appearance and self-presentation, in which the necktie has played a significant part, is elemental to sociality. We may

[3] The story is interesting for its modern resonances. To explain, for example, that the popularity of blue jeans can be connected to the American Levi Strauss, or that Ray Kroc invented the fast food restaurant and the original McDonald's, is to identify a single individual as a social catalyst. Such explanations parallel the authenticating narrative of the consumer-oriented industrial societies which emphasize an ethic of individualism. As an explanation of a social event, the nomenclature of the authenticating narrative cannot be fully accepted because it works simultaneously at the epistemological levels of fact, fiction and interpretation.

devalue fashionability as an accessory to sociation, but the endurance of the idea that character is integral to, and can be read from, appearance, renders fashion important. Quentin Bell has quoted a letter dated November 1745 from Lord Chesterfield to his son advising him to take fashions seriously; 'Dress is a very foolish thing; yet it is a very foolish thing for a man not to be well dressed' (Chesterfield in Bell 1976:18).

Fashions are bonds that link individuals in a mutual act of conformity to social conventions. In this manner, fashion constitutes a popular language through which many individuals publicly represent themselves. In the twentieth century, this appears to make fashion a democratic language. There are, after all, few restrictions on dress, and those in operation are mainly concerned with ensuring gender differences and occupational identities. In these ways, fashionability is employed, in the course of the everyday, to ease sociation; it can allow for certain customs to be violated, say, cross-dressing or pretending to wear garments of great value but which are, instead, imitations such as fake furs, vinyl-leather jackets, plastic tortoiseshell and costume jewellery. In these instances, there is little risk of severe rebuke. However, fashionability is not entirely benign; there are certain codes which cannot be broken without consequence. For example, when men in business fail to wear a necktie with a suit, or when women wear trousers at traditional events such as regal receptions, then customary styles of social exchange will be jeopardized. The offending individual may be considered unbalanced, aspersions against his or her character might be made and social pressures toward changing his or her appearance, drawing it into closer conformity with others, will be enacted. In contemporary dress styles there is a certain degree of flexibility; for example, men have a much larger casual wardrobe of clothes than they did two decades ago, and this gives a greater sense of freedom. Furthermore, there are few legal injunctions such as sumptuary laws which determine styles of dress; although it may be illegal to wear the uniforms of certain occupational groups, such as the police force, few people find the legal constraint to be a serious limitation on their style of appearance. Irrespective of these freedoms in clothing styles, fashionability has become a crucial influence on the modern individual's physical appearance. It plays a significant role in supporting social customs and expectations in obvious and commonplace ways such as with styles of appearance that are gender and age appropriate. The fashionability of the necktie is assured in the modern world. It is a staple of men's fashion clothing, 'an adornment much like a piece of jewellery' and it is frequently worn as a 'method of self-expression' which advertises the taste, character and sensibilities of the wearer.[4] It is noteworthy that a decorative item such as the necktie has become a credential of the wearer's seriousness and respectability. As such, a sliver of material resting on a man's chest has become expressive of a number of cultural ideals and social values. At the same time, the symbolic value of the necktie can be parodied and imitated. Indeed, in the manufacture of the necktie, the ingredients of pretence are already built in.

To produce a necktie, a dozen or more procedures are involved. To begin, the material is cut, a process that requires varying degrees of skill depending on the kind of material. The sturdier the material, the easier and quicker the cut, thus, the leather tie is the easiest. Similarly, artificial fabrics such as acetates and polyesters, which are also relatively sturdy, are easy to style, but silk, particularly crêpe de chine, is extremely difficult to shape. Subsequently, the silk tie has to be hand-stitched, making it more expensive to produce. The cost of production and the retail value of the tie vary according to prevailing fashions, but a general estimate is that the costs of manufacture are less than one-fifth of the retail value.

As with most mass-produced goods, the manufacturing process has made items cheaper and increased the market demand. With the necktie, this is also the case; a machine now performs most steps in the manufacturing process. After the material is cut by a skilled cutter, a machine can be used to join and press

[4] These are the views of the executive director of Brummell Ties (a fictitious name), a manufacturing firm which produces more than two hundred dozen ties per day and successfully markets the product throughout the southern hemisphere. The information about the manufacture and costs of the necktie is also from this source.

the seams of each piece of cloth. At this stage, the tie resembles a jigsaw piece with asymmetrical flaps and panels. The next step is to style the tie into its conventional shape beginning with the tip. It is at the tip of the tie, which is always visible, that the tie's quality is most immediately apparent, it is here where corrugations and curls can readily occur, thus hampering the flow of the suspended tie and destroying its most alluring characteristic. The best ties are edged with a fine mitre that holds the tip at a precise angle. When the tip of the tie is formed and the lining inserted, the tie is turned out or reversed to reveal its final face. These stages can now be performed mechanically.

The wearing of a necktie is a study in the economics of personal bearing. The point of wearing a tie is its value as a status symbol. The more status it can appear to express, the greater its value. So, ties that suggest links with the establishment or exclusive club memberships are supposedly more impressive; the same with ties which appear intrinsically valuable, such as the silk tie and its imitations. The manner of wearing a tie also reflects status. Wearing a tie that creates a distraction, that is frequently in need of adjustment and realignment of position, detracts from its social value. The tie must be worn as if it were a natural appendage: from its pivot at the throat, the tie should hang along the body as if it belonged. Thus, the status generated by the tie is paralleled by its unobtrusiveness. The stiff tie, say, the leather tie, needs to be restrained with a stud or clip, otherwise it builds momentum independent of the wearer. However, to restrain the stiff tie with a stud or clip is to produce other detractions such as unsightly buckling when the wearer sits. In contrast, the light silk tie adheres more readily to other materials and takes on a fluid complementarity with the wearer's other garments, but the lighter tie still has its difficulties. Its textural lightness may require fixing to the shirt and, at such times, it evidences the same problems as the fixed stiff tie, namely, that it can loop and buckle.

Ties are similar to other items of conspicuous consumption, such as pieces of jewellery, in that they have great social value but little practical use. As Veblen (1899) noted a century earlier, the conspicuous display of valued goods has little to do with comfort, utility or ease of movement, but has much to do with assertions of status and power. The necktie may appear a frippery of attire but, like other adornments, it has been made into an assertion of identity and social status. That an item as decorative as the tie can be read as a representation of character, that abstract human qualities have become embedded in material objects, brings attention to the muted discourse and the embedded, ambiguous and unexplicated ways in which we understand and talk of personal identity and character, at the present time.

Davis (1985) claims that modern identity is in a state of constant flux and that we attempt to order it by following, in our appearance and conduct, well-publicized guidelines such as fashions. However, this is paradoxical; the directives that fashion seems to offer are little more than inducements to continue in a search which has no end. The continual changes we observe in the material conditions of the modern world impinge upon us to destabilize any sense of continuity we may have. Thus, our sense of personal identity is being constantly unhinged; as Davis has described:

(We are) prodded by social and technological change, the biological decrements of the life cycle, visions of utopia, and occasions of disaster, our identities are forever in ferment giving rise to numerous strains, paradoxes, ambivalences and contradictions within ourselves. It is upon these collectively experienced, sometimes historically recurrent identity instabilities that fashion feeds. (1985:24)

In the modern era, clothing has become less formalistic, and so the risks of misreading the character of the other from it have increased. At the same time, clothing is more regimented by fashionability, so more people begin to look alike and wear items of a similar kind. Clothing can be used as a silent description of the other, especially so with uniforms and exclusive garments such as those associated with gender, or the ceremonial garb of public office, or the uniforms of civic functionaries. There are as well widely known icons like lipstick, hose, earrings, business suits, neckties and so on, which announce primary statuses of the individual and predict the types of

127

engagement that might be encountered when so attired. Thus, males and females have clear rules governing appearance: most males wear business suits with a shirt and tie, most females wear dresses or skirts with stockings and heeled shoes. Some professions have uniforms; the constabulary, judiciary, laboratory scientist, technician, hospital nurse and so on are easily recognized. Other occupations are so thoroughly gendered that we expect a secretary, sales assistant and office worker to be female and to be clad in a dress. In some instances, we are prepared to accept deviations to a certain degree, such as doctors dressed in tweeds reminiscent of the landed gentry, and university academics in the corporate business suit. We accept these deviations because we know that styles in clothing can be social disguises or masks behind which the individual wants to feel concealed. We have also accepted that clothing styles can create confusion, say, when cross-dressing occurs. Even so, these deviations and exceptions do not weaken the idea that clothing can be suggestive of human character. Indeed, these anomalous instances in clothing styles more often reinforce the axiom that we use appearance to reflect character because in instances where we are mistaken or misled we are forced to see the ubiquity of the assumption that character can be fashioned by appearances.

Our mistakes in reading character from appearance rarely deter us; paradoxically, our mistakes seem to support the view that appearances are important and that our fashioning of a convincing, appealing or arresting appearance is an effective means of influencing the other. In cases of error, we learn that we need to improve our perceptual reading of the other. When we encounter the stranger as initially mysterious and inaccessible, we refer to clothing styles and physical appearance, in the absence of any other means, as a reliable sign of identity. Clothing is frequently seen as symbolic of the individual's status and morality, whether actual or contrived. In an era dominated by conspicuous consumption, where we are continuously enjoined to accept the new, the changing and the fashionable as if they were valuable commodities, it is not surprising that a continual re-fashioning of the body, and our physical appearance, should be commonplace. Undergirding this continual refurbishment may be the embedded desire to make the self richer, more complex, more appealing, in the same manner that we have learned to think of objects being continually improved by their re-design. In the next chapter, where the effect of fashionability on social relations is discussed, these ideas are given more attention.

5

Fashionability

Fashionability is an essential ingredient in the successful mass distribution of consumerables. It is fashionability that enables a commodity to be sold and resold in slightly different form many times over, and it is the constant reselling of the chameleonic object that generates much of the wealth of an industrialized economy. From the previous chapter, where the case of the ordinary necktie, a purely decorative item of clothing, illustrated the economic aspects of fashion and personal bearing, it is clear that the capitalization of fashions is without par, and that any analysis of fashion cannot avoid its economic character. However, studying fashion as a primarily economic phenomenon is not sufficient. Fashionability has a decisive influence upon social relations. Fashion is a means by which images of the self can be created and displayed. With the expansion of the fashion industries, a greater diversity in styles of appearance has evolved so that we can now act in the public domain as if we each possessed a multiplicity of identities; in the course of a day, with each change of outfit and venue of activity, we can appear to be a slightly different person. Fashion has made styles in appearance into proclamations of proclivities, capacities and personality. This is a unique feature of our social life; as Sontag (1966:18) has remarked of modern

130

times, 'our manner of appearing *is* our manner of being. The mask is the face.'

Veblen's nineteenth-century analysis of fashion rested firmly upon an economic base and the assumed universality of conspicuous consumption. He maintained that 'no class of society, not even the most abjectly poor, foregoes all customary conspicuous consumption' (Veblen 1899:85). At the same time, Veblen did recognize that influences other than economics were also at work and that the practices of conspicuous consumption were related to the moral fabric of a community. Later commentators, such as Simmel (1904), Flügel (1930), Blumer (1969), Fraser (1981), Barthes (1985), Davis (1985), Eckstein and Firkins (1987), also acknowledged the economics of fashion, but then proceeded to invoke other elements in its explanation. The act of conspicuously consuming goods and the idea of fashionability behind these acts have become prosaic parts of everyday consciousness, part of the authenticating narrative that makes self-display and self-characterization seem the most natural of social activities. Much of this chapter is directed towards examining the effect that fashionability, conspicuous consumption and the commodification of personal identity have on social relations and on the individual's sense of self.

Fashions in clothing and appearance bring attention to the body and to particular parts of the body. Certain styles of dress emphasize parts of the body which, in turn, speak of other designations; the necktie, as we have previously seen, draws an imaginery line along the torso between the throat and the pelvis, directing attention to the physical features of masculinity. Barthes's (1985) account of décolletage provides another example where the characteristics of the body are adamantly defined by clothing; in this instance, a woman's neck and shoulders are emphasized by the shape of the dress, thereby contributing to the definition of modern femininity. Appearance, Banner (1983:3) has similarly reported, is commonly considered a primary mark of personal identification used by both women and men as a declaration of what they consider themselves to be. This idea would explain the allegiance of many women to those styles and fashions which require physical exertion or prolonged discomfort, even pain, such as narrow stiletto shoes, the tight-laced corset and the surgical reshaping of the face and body in accord with prevailing styles. The individual's tolerance of these demands indicates the importance of the 'right' appearance.

Many fashions alter the shape of the body, sometimes irreversibly, in order to bring the individual into a closer alignment with prevailing ideals of physical attractiveness. Kunzle (1982), Banner (1983) and Steele (1985) have each suggested that the meaning of the nineteenth-century women's habit of tight-lacing, which strenuously reshaped the waist, hips and bosom into an hour-glass silhouette, was related to how successfully this mode of appearance equated with prevailing definitions of beauty, femininity and women's social status. The practice was opposed by nineteenth-century dress reformers, feminists and some medical practitioners, whose collective injunctions may have had an influence in diminishing its popularity (Banner 1983:47–8, 86–93). However, that the fashion endured for so long underscores the wider argument that character was accepted as being evidenced through one's physical appearance, in this case, that feminine qualities were expressed by the hour-glass figure. The way one appears has, for a long time and across various cultural distinctions, remained of fundamental importance to the individual's sense of identity.

It may seem as if fashions in appearance function primarily to represent gender differences, especially in Western culture. Fashions seem to have perennially contrasted the appropriate styles for men and women, such as trousers for men and skirts for women. At the same time, there are many styles of clothing where differences between men and women's attire are negligible, including the occasional fad for unisex (Laver 1969:7).

The separation of the sexes is repeatedly performed in marketing strategies because it increases the number of arenas in which a product can be sold. Both Roberts (1977) and McCracken (1985) have independently identified the features of male and female attire which have operated throughout the nineteenth and twentieth centuries as the means for distinguishing these two market groups. Both of them have emphasized how effective were distinctive styles of clothing, and they continue to be, as structural agents which reinforce conventional sex roles. The specific characteristics relate to colour, style and fabric. Men's clothing has generally been of darker colours, often monochromatic, to symbolize the seriousness of their social position. This dulling of appearance began in the early nineteenth century in parallel with the development of the business economy (de Marly 1985). It seemed that a new sobriety in appearance was propitious in the commercial domain to elicit a sense of trust and cooperation from the prospective client and co-worker alike. Men's clothing has come to be tailored in an angular, square mode using stiff, sturdy and durable material allowing for a great deal of physical movement. Male clothing has come to be relatively unadorned; there is little ornamentation to catch the eye or draw one's attention. In stark contrast, conventional female clothing creates an opposite effect; women wear clothes of lighter, softer materials which are more varied in colour. The style of tailoring is less exact, there are curves, drops, flowing lines and an amalgamation of textures; a more elaborate styling of the costume often means greater changes in the overall shape and the effect has been to curtail bodily movement. Commonly, female clothing is adorned with trimmings of ribbon and lace, there are pieces of jewellery, ornaments and accessories which create a frivolous effect and draw attention to specific parts of the body (Roberts 1977:556; McCracken 1985:46). In a time when the beauty of the body is the female's greatest social asset, clothing has been designed to accentuate it (Banner 1983).

Currently, as women enter the male-dominated arenas of law, government, commerce and so on, their dress has taken on masculine characteristics (Molloy 1975; 1977). The traditional business uniform of men, usually in a block, neutral colour with 'the necktie that adds a touch of color and (is) the means for transmitting minor social messages' (Fraser 1981:232–3), has recently been modified for women. Women, in certain professions, have made the business suit their uniform as well;

but, to Kennedy Fraser's practised eye, women's suits, like their performances in the jobs, are different to those of men. She has commented that women in business

> still have to be slightly more than men in equivalent positions – slightly harder-working, slightly brighter, slightly more self-protective, perhaps even slightly more aggressive. And they feel impelled to give far more attention to looking well dressed. The suggested fashions for women in business begin with the uniform of men in business – the suit – and then add touches of self-consciousness, or even self-parody. (1981:232)

These touches are 'exaggeratedly feminine accessories' such as hats, eye-catching gloves, recklessly high and thin stiletto heels and jewellery (Fraser 1981:228). The form of fashion that has evolved for women in business is designed to fit into the world of men (1981:227), so there are feminized neckties and bowties to accompany the female suit. The traditional and exclusive male accoutrements of the cuff-links, fob watch and waistcoat have also become at times fashionable female accessories (Eckstein and Firkins 1987:5). These examples indicate how important is appearance to the identity that the individual wishes to claim.

Following the idea that personal appearance and fashionability are commonly used to broadcast self-image, women imitating conventional male attire may be thought of as signalling their ambitions for the same achievements and statuses held by modern men. At the same time, the reverse of the idea can also be seen at work; that in men's increasing interest in the vagaries of fashion, for example, their adoption of frivolous items such as silk shirts with embroidery on the breast pocket, jewellery and ornamentation, there is a suggestion that the social value and status of the male as primary worker is changing. If we accept that fashions in appearance reflect self-evaluations, then men's increasing concern over their appearance and their acceptance of an element of flamboyance in it may be predictive of a change, perhaps a decline, in their social value as workers in the post-industrial economy.

A further indication of this can be discerned in the relatively new male cosmetic industry (*Cosmetics and Toiletries Report* 1985). The small number of after-shave lotions have now been augmented with male colognes, fresheners, lotions, blockouts and tinted face creams. Indeed, many of the products are those long used by women but now repackaged and marketed with different, more masculinized names. Fraser has noted that men now have a greater interest in 'the promises of the cosmetics industry' (Fraser 1981:249), including surgical procedures such as hair treatments and face lifts. Cosmetics for men exemplify how commonly products are duplicated in order to tap into a new market; that is, rather than developing new products, changes are made to an existing product's associated image. The ability to market the same commodity to both women and men – although such a commodity is packaged differently – means that investing goods with gender identifications has proved to be a lucrative market strategy. While it is the case that the mass production of clothing and the democratization of fashion have been well established as an economic means of producing goods, it is also important to note that the marketing of these items has been greatly enhanced by separating objects into female and male versions. The same commodity, whether it be an automobile, blue jeans, perfume, socks, furniture and so on, can be styled, advertised, sold and defined twice over as it were, when it is fashioned into either a female or male symbol. The success of such commodity differentiation indicates the high social premium attached to the individual's identification with either the masculine or feminine.

Modern fashions in clothing and appearance do more than assert gender, even though gender distinctions may seem their most obvious effect. Other social statuses being expressed pertain to class, self-image and social aspirations. Davis (1985) has argued that styles of clothing, irrespective of their fashionability, are strongly attached to social identity. Clothing is employed, in part, as a means for claiming an identity within the public arena. Of course, the idea that dress and identity are interwoven long predates any commercial development of the fashion industries. In the *Odyssey*, Athene transformed Odysseus by altering his physical shape and clothing so he could escape his identity and enjoy the freedom of anonymity. By

135

disguising him as a dirty, dishevelled old man, Athene provided Odysseus with the means to remain unrecognized; '(Athene) shrivelled the lovely flesh on his supple limbs, destroyed the blond hair on his head, and put the skin of an aged old man around all his limbs ... She threw other clothing about him; a foul rag and a tunic, dirty and full of holes' (Homer 1974:184–5). Even when Odysseus' wife Penelope knew that the old, shrivelled man was her husband, still the outer appearance, and the unfamiliar clothing, prevented her recognizing him; 'with her gaze sometimes she looked him full in the face, and sometimes did not know him for the vile clothes he had on his skin' (Homer 1974:313).

Clearly, physical appearances are understood to do more than differentiate the sexes; they act as social passports and credentials, often speaking out more eloquently than the individual might desire. In Odysseus' case, he must transform himself in order to gain the social freedom he required. His appearance is a passport to other social realms. In the following example from Primo Levi, appearances are used as a credential of one's humanity. In his document of the Nazi concentration camps, *If This Be A Man* (1987), Levi described an episode where an inmate of Auschwitz, L, understood even in the torturous circumstances of the camps, that there was power to be gained through deliberately fashioning one's appearance. L went to extreme lengths to cultivate his appearance, so, in the barbaric conditions of the concentration camp where everyone was soiled and fouled, his hands and face were always perfectly clean, and his striped prison suit was also 'clean and new': 'L knew that the step was short from being judged powerful to effectively becoming so ... a respectable appearance is the best guarantee of being respected ... He needed no more than his spruce suit and his emaciated and shaved face in the midst of the flock of his sordid and slovenly colleagues' to stand out and thereby receive benefits from his captors (Levi 1987:100–1).

The recognition of appearance as a basic element in sociality has long been enshrined in the idea of the sumptuary laws. These laws, which governed the conventions of appearance in Europe, mainly, between the thirteenth and seventeenth centuries, were in existence well before the rise of the fashion industries. Sumptuary laws were designed to govern styles in clothing and set limits on ownership of valued goods in order to preserve the social hierarchy. Sumptuary laws were aimed at ensuring that with a glance at attire, individuals could recognize the social station of others. Throughout history, distinctions have been made in the styles of dress and trimmings permitted for wear by different groups such as the peasantry, the lesser bourgeoisie, those in industry and trade, chancery officials, clerks, knights and nobles, doctors and licentiates, counts, barons and so on (von Boehn 1932: vol. 3, 170). In France, in 1294, by decree of Philippe le Bel, no one but the nobility could own or wear grey furs, ermine or gold; in 1362, by decree of Edward III, the English merchant was permitted to dress in the same way as the aristocracy, but only when a merchant's income exceeded a noble's by fivefold. Thus, the merchant worth a thousand pounds a year could dress as did the knight on two hundred pounds a year. In 1463 Edward IV declared that purple silk was to be the prerogative of the aristocracy; in 1510 Henry VIII restricted the amount of cloth to be used in garments (de Marly 1985:19–21).

At various times sumptuary laws have provided detailed descriptions of how individuals could appear in public, and how they could conduct themselves, particularly with regard to the right to own and display valued materials. Sumptuary laws used items of apparel and specialized goods as emblematic of social status. They made the social and political character of a society evident through the distribution of material resources. Thus, individuals could understand, at a glance, the power and position of the other. Social identity was immediately communicable; the other would only be mysterious or threatening when these outward signs of position were confused, or did not conform to the customs of the day. In this manner, sumptuary laws were representations of the political and social hierarchy of a society, and their purposes were not only to identify individuals to one another but, also, to regulate certain kinds of economic and social conduct. Frequently, the prohibited items singled out by sumptuary laws were expensive items central to the organization of a society's economy. For example, in the fourteenth century, when Edward III decreed that no foreign cloth was to be imported into England, he was concerned more with the protection of home industries than with any current debates about fashion and aesthetic appearance. In instances where the ownership of gold, jewels and furs was confined to royalty or members of the court, the prohibition had much to do with preserving the social order by guarding against the accumulation of too much wealth by those who might challenge the status quo. Elias (1982) and Williams (1982) have each described how conspicuous consumption was encouraged in the French court as a device to dissipate wealth that may otherwise have been used to finance acts of opposition and challenges to the prevailing rule. These displays of wealth by court members were dictated by the dynamics of the political situation; they were not engaged in, nor were they understood as gestures of individuality, as we might understand them in the late twentieth century. As Williams (1982:30) has described, 'The routine of the court demonstrates how a system of consumption can develop its own imperatives, which bear little relation to the attainment of individual happiness or even pleasure.'

Sumptuary laws were techniques for preserving the status quo but, at the same time, they did exert an influence over habits of daily commerce. In so far as these laws could determine which styles in physical appearance were customary and which material objects and goods were of value, then they controlled, in effect, the social distribution of wealth. Sumptuary laws were a conservative influence, they bolstered the conventions and customs of the day by regulating the acquisition and exchange of valuable goods. At the same time, these laws were technically unenforceable, which meant that their power resided in the willingness of individuals to accept the importance of appearance. For instance, imposing sumptuary laws on the dressing practices of individuals in private was impossible: who could prevent the rich merchant wearing the restricted or prohibited purple silk in his own home? Certainly, the adherence to these laws by the majority of the population was more a function of there being little opportunity to do otherwise; that is, the market in fine clothes and the costs of tailoring restricted luxury and fashionable attire to a small section of the society. Nevertheless, the prominence of these laws also speaks to an enduring belief in the power of physical appearance. The individual's appearance has been eloquent – clothing and adornments have the power to describe the system of stratification of a society and its permutations.

In the industrialized societies of the twentieth century, where the fashion industries are well established, public restrictions and regulations of appearance seem largely non-existent. There are some restrictions in occupational clothing, such as military, medical and sporting uniforms, judicial and academic robes, ecclesiastical raiment and so on, and these function as did sumptuary laws to alert individuals to certain proscriptive modes of conduct. One would certainly find oneself acting and speaking differently to the other when s/he was clad in the uniform of the constabulary, or clothed in ecclesiastical or judicial robes. However, in general, public appearance is ungoverned by explicit laws and, importantly, this means that styles in dress cannot always be used with full confidence as a measure of the individual's social location. Indeed, clothes, when used as ostentatious symbols of class and status (see Packard 1959), may well be used to mislead and misrepresent. This unreliability of a correspondence between the individual's dress and social identity was well illustrated by Veblen.

Veblen's analysis of the leisure class was also a study in the meaning of fashion and the ways in which fashionability made the stratification of modern society more convoluted. He described how members of the upper class, in late nineteenth-century America, were preoccupied with the display of their newly acquired wealth. Fashionability was a device for publicizing social status. The new nineteenth-century upper class consumed products and pursued pleasures as conspicuously as possible. They made their tastes in material possessions and their personal proclivities into representations of power and status. Frangible objects, fashionable clothing, items of luxury and wealth were transformed into claims of social superiority, so that social leadership and prominence became a function of conspicuous consumption and conspicuous waste. The dynamic behind this conduct was economic. The value of an object or practice was a function of its exclusivity and cost. Being conspicuously fashionable, pursuing exclusive activities, continually adopting new styles and habits were the trademarks of the upper class and assertions of an elevated social position. When members of the lower classes emulated these styles, those in the upper class immediately abandoned them. This mode of behaviour was in contradiction to the ethic of parsimony shown by an earlier generation of American pioneers and settlers. In the nineteenth century, Veblen recorded the new habit that to waste goods and squander time were now acceptable, even enviable, indications of wealth.

Veblen's theory of social stratification was accurate enough for that moment of late nineteenth-century America when the mechanisms of capital accumulation were expanding without hindrance. The limitations of Veblen's theory stem from his reading of human nature, specifically, from his idea that it is imitation and differentiation which are the oxymoronic principles guiding all human conduct. Veblen argued that as the upper class constantly differentiated itself from the lower class by defining and redefining the fashionable, the lower class continually imitated the fashions that 'trickled down' the social ladder and, in turn, this propelled the upper class to invent and produce further goods and insignia of distinction. The character of the society was one of a continuous cycle of development and abandonment of social habits and valued possessions. This account of social stratification required an ever-expanding industrial and manufacturing sphere in which the new fancies of the upper classes could always be rapidly produced. Further, it rested upon the assumption of there being two well-defined classes, upper and lower, and that these two classes existed in continuous repudiation of each other.

Such an account is limited to a short period of America's economic history. After Veblen, Henry Ford's mass manufacture of the monochromatic Tin Lizzie motor car completely altered the dynamic established by imitation and differentiation. Veblen's theory was no longer convincing in the circumstances where consumer items became more widely available and cheaper to purchase. The revolutionary idea behind Henry Ford's new car was that items produced by new manufacturing processes should be affordable by those individuals who laboured in their production. Greater fortunes could be made when conspicuous consumption was enjoyed by greater numbers of people; Ford could become richer after the Tin Lizzie made the luxury of a car democratically available to everyone.

In the late twentieth century, a number of other factors have meant that Veblen's characterization of social life as a continual exchange of imitation and differentiation between the lower and upper classes is far too narrow. These factors include the expansion of fashion to include all manner of goods and services, the ecological and technological problems of industrial growth in the capitalist societies, the blurring of class boundaries and the plundering of subcultures for novel commodities. However, with these dramatic economic shifts in mind, there are elements of Veblen's theory, in particular, the ease with which fashionable items can be made into emblems of the individual's power and distinction, which maintain his importance and explain his influence on later theorists such as Simmel.

Simmel (1904) followed much of Veblen's economic account of social stratification but he also recognized that fashions need not be restricted to economic commodities. Fashion could exert an influence on the sociality of individuals, including the manners that regulated human exchange and the ideas which fuelled human activity. As Simmel stated, 'social forms, apparel, aesthetic judgement, the whole style of human expression, are constantly transformed by fashion' (1904:299). With this claim, Simmel extended the orbit of fashionability beyond clothing and personal adornment to include the general demeanour of individuals, their tastes in art, leisure activities and choice of civic duties. To apply the dynamics of fashion beyond the economic sphere, as Simmel has done, and to suggest that the manners and habits of the individual's ordinary life may be subject to the same impulses as fashion, is to claim, audaciously, that fashionability and conspicuous consumption are elemental parts of the individual's inner life. As Simmel has stated:

> It may also be considered a sign of the increased power of fashion, that it has overstepped the bounds of its original domain,

141

which comprised only personal externals, and has acquired an increasing influence over taste, over theoretical convictions, and even over the moral foundations of life. (1904:303–4)

With this view, Simmel provided the idea of fashion with architectonic dimensions. He suggested, firstly, that fashionability had the capacity to structure the physical world; thus, it was a force in defining what was aesthetically pleasing, say, in the design of houses, cars, office buildings and works of art. Secondly, Simmel's view suggested that fashions could shape the interior world of the individual by establishing thresholds of sentiments that classified what was repugnant and appealing in ideas, practices and desires. Importantly, fashions could shape the mannerisms common to social conduct such as expressions of modesty, embarrassment, self-consciousness, superiority, confidence, ambition, even a concern for others. Sentiments, no less than material commodities, were shaped by fashions, and as Simmel pointed out, it was in this way that the inner life of the individual became subject to external interests; 'fashion can to all appearances and *in abstracto* absorb any chosen content: any given form of clothing, of art, of conduct, of opinion may become fashionable' (Simmel 1904:321).

Simmel recognized that fashionability constituted an important element in modern life, indeed, a significant characteristic of modernity was the growing influence that fashion and its effects had upon moral foundations, on what was considered personally proper and societally progressive (Simmel 1904:303–4). For Simmel, fashion legitimated an ethic of constant change. Fashion reinforced the idea that normative conduct – in dress or ideas – was contingent on circumstances, and what was acceptable and natural at one time would not be at another. The mentality promulgated by fashionability saw morality as a contingency, as never being finally or eternally established.

The modern era has been dominated by an ethic of contingency. Simmel argued that the modern individual could not help but be overwhelmed by the diversity of opportunities, amusements and activities found in metropolitan life. The proliferation of the material culture had been so rapid and comprehensive that the individual must inevitably fail to understand, or even to observe, all that existed about him or her. The success of technology and mass manufacturing had created such an abundance of material goods that the individual must inevitably feel overwhelmed by the colossal physical proportions of the world. In such an atmosphere, where the individual may feel dominated and even threatened with obliteration, an acute desire for differentiation and singularity becomes more pressing. Thus, it happens that a dynamic is set in motion in which the diminution of the individual is countered by a desire for individuality and it is fashion which appears to the individual, at this point, as a socially benign means of providing that sense of individuality.

Much of the value of being fashionable rests upon the successful eliciting of the other's envy and admiration; by being fashionable the individual seeks to be more than the other (Simmel 1950:343). The idea is that we are somehow enlarged by demonstrations of material and pecuniary strength; 'the radiations of adornment, the sensuous attention it provokes, supply the personality with such an enlargement or intensification of its sphere; the personality, so to speak, is more when it is adorned' (Simmel 1950:340). From the psychoanalytic tradition, Flügel has observed much the same, that fashion promises to increase the stature of the individual; 'clothing, by adding to the apparent size of the body in one way or another, gives us an increased sense of power, a sense of extension of our bodily self' (Flügel 1930:34). Fashion can be the reflection of a desire to elicit envy from the other and, in this way, to gain distinctiveness (Flügel 1930:138–40). Simmel has pointed out that the value of fashion lies with its being an expression of a personal desire for differentiation and distinction in a world that threatens to overwhelm us – 'the individual desires to distinguish himself before others, and to be the object of an attention that others do not receive' (Simmel 1950:338). Being fashionable is a means by which the individual can exaggerate him or herself, thereby, making him or herself audible above the cacophony of metropolitan life (Simmel 1950:422).

Paradoxically, there is another aspect to fashion which undercuts and fails to meet these needs for distinctiveness. By

143

being fashionable, the individual relinquishes the opportunity to think about how best to represent him or herself to others. Allegiance to fashion replaces the need to examine one's style of public conduct and, instead, one has merely to be obedient to the prevailing conventions. In this way, a consequence of fashionability is that it diminishes the individual's sense of stature and distinctiveness. As Simmel (1904:323) has stated, 'fashion releases the individual from ethical and aesthetic responsibility by requiring the individual to act like others.' Fashion requires imitation and that, in turn, has the effect of binding us more closely to the other. As Simmel has described:

> (Fashion) gives to the individual the satisfaction of not standing alone in his (*sic*) actions. Whenever we imitate, we transfer not only the demand for creative ability, but also the responsibility for the action from ourselves to another. Thus the individual is freed from the worry of choosing and appears simply as a creature of the group, as a vessel of the social contents. (1904:295)

The fashionable individual is thus more intelligible to the other, more easily recognized and more readily socially placed. The irony is that the fashionable individual may feel as if s/he stands out more and is more distinctive because 'in the adorned body, we possess more', as Simmel has stated (1950:344), but being fashionable makes one more common and conventional, more readily interpretable. The paradox is that in the mass society which utilizes the desire for personal distinctiveness to propel its members toward increased conspicuous consumption, there is less societal value placed on being distinctive. In the late twentieth century, the dynamic of fashionability promises individuality in an historical epoch where individuality is neither economically valued nor socially useful. Indeed, real individuality is more often disparaged as eccentricity. The irony of seeing fashionability as a solution to the problem of identity is that fashions do not distinguish individuals; on the contrary, fashions embed and integrate the individual into society.

It is possible to conclude from Simmel that the modern individual has a feeble sense of identity (Simmel 1950:409–11) because a life which is commonly passed amidst a plethora of material goods, as in the industrialized twentieth century, is a life in which the need to choose this object or that line of activity, on a basis other than that of fashion, is unwanted. The abundance of objects and activities preempts the necessity for much considered thought about the value and satisfaction we expect to derive from their purchase or pursuit. After all, it does not matter whether we choose to do this or that, to do it now or later, because there will always be another series, at another time, of what appear to be choices and options. The abundance of choice has meant in effect that there are no contrasting options, only an endless array of commodities, amusements and engagements.

The internalized experience of fashionability and commodity consumption is interwoven with ambiguities and contradictions. In a world of abundance where objects and practices are continually circulating, we may well experience a subliminal sense of uneasiness because we can never be sure of the social longevity of the interests and tastes we have chosen to pursue. Having an abundance of goods and products seems to diminish their value. Thus, our desire to secure from fashionability a sense of personal uniqueness or distinction is virtually impossible because of the perennial fluctuations in value and pleasure associated with fashionable items. Indeed, our pursuit of fashion as a source of personal identity is, paradoxically, the primary ingredient in the degradation of identity. After all, if we are relying upon the properties of procured goods for our sense of identity, then we are compelled to procure again and again.

Fashion, by its capacity to structure the everyday world and order interpersonal commerce in a way that emphasizes the surface life, constitutes an insidious attack on the ability to reflect on the meaning of our desires. As a system of discourse, fashion always emphasizes the importance of the new, and this has provided the individual with a prefigured social universe in which s/he is relieved of the need to examine, analyse or judge any of the elements of that universe. Thus, individuals engaged by fashions have little opportunity to develop either reflective or intellectual capacities; fashionability engenders an ethic of contingency in which everything is made relative to the prevailing customs and images of the moment; this has the consequence of deflating any importance which may come to be attached to the kinds of reflection and sociality which endure through time.

Poggioli (1968:111) has reached much the same point with his argument that the modern era has become a 'culture of negation' because of its domination by material abundancy and fashionability. Poggioli has pointed out that when a culture is constantly remade by a series of disruptions, disjunctions, changes and overturnings, as is the case with the ever-fluctuating cycles of fashion, then social discontinuity becomes institutionalized as the norm.

> The chief characteristic of fashion is to impose and suddenly to accept as a new rule or norm what was, until a minute before, an exception or whim, then to abandon it again after it has become a commonplace, everybody's 'thing'. Fashion's task, in brief, is to maintain a continual process of standardisation: putting a rarity or novelty into general and universal use, then passing on to another rarity or novelty when the first has ceased to be such. (1968:79)

Fashion has become a major source of personal identification; in effect, this has meant that we have learned to value the image of how we appear to be, how we are styled. This is the fashioned self. Like the physiognomists, it places emphasis upon appearance, although the appearance in this instance has been cultivated and shaped by a maze of extraneous influences. In effect, fashion has elevated the surface life of appearances into a dominant influence on sociality; thus, what may be privately thought of as a distinctive form of individualistic expression is, in actuality, the opposite, namely, the adoption of a widely publicized image, the ideals of the authenticating narrative of our time.

Barthes (1985) has argued that an effect of fashionability is to heighten the individual's sense of the immediate and to weaken the sense of the past and future. Fashion fixes the individual to the present, with a concomitant loss in the ability to step beyond the obvious and the immediate to evaluate the actions

5 Fashionability

being followed. This is, Barthes has stated 'the natural right of the present over the past' (1985:273). Fashions are constantly absorbing and elevating the demands of the present moment over those of a past which, by definition, are dead, irrelevant and unimportant: 'fashion is never anything but an amnesiac substitution of the present for the past' (Barthes 1985:289). Simmel (1971:303) has said much the same; 'fashion always occupies the dividing-line between the past and the future, and consequently conveys a stronger feeling of the present ... than most other phenomena.'

It is in this way that being fashionable appears to offer the individual a degree of control over his or her immediate circumstances, so that it seems by adopting a particular fashion the individual can be 'everything at once, without having to choose' (Barthes 1985:255). Thus, an appeal of fashionability is its promise both to reveal and promote aspects of a new persona in the individual; fashionability promises to emancipate the individual from the customary and, thereby, enrich the self. By adding new styles in the repertoire of the individual's appearance, it seems as if fashionability teases out the wisps and tendrils of a self-identity which might otherwise have remained dormant or repressed. In echo of Simmel's observation that the adorned body has greater stature, the self is, thus, thought to be enlarged by fashion because fashion seems to call upon the self to shift continuously, to reshape itself to embrace and accommodate the new. Thus, being fashionable creates the illusion that one has a great deal of control and self-determinism.

To speculate on what it may mean in terms of our modern mentality and, in particular, to the manners of social life, that the ethic of fashionability extends beyond the material sphere to reach into the common stock of knowledge and moral code of the individual, is to reach a conclusion consonant with Simmel's, namely, that modern social life is of tragic proportions (Simmel 1971). Modern social relations, and the sense of self that is leached from them, are an abnegation of our cultural ideals of human character. For instance, the existence of fashion elevates the public realm over that of the private; it emphasizes the surface of everyday life and obvious elements

147

such as styles in appearance and fashionability. Along with this emphasis comes a diminution in importance of those traits such as taste, critique and judgement which require lengthy cultivation and are the products of a reflexive sociality. Fashion, in its capacity to mediate human relations through an abbreviated language and code of meanings and images, illustrates how the sensibilities and intellectuality of the modern individual can be reduced by social forms (in this instance, fashions) which are themselves narrow in meaning. Using commodities or fashions to mediate social relations means that an externalization of interests is occurring; fashion objects become icons that direct social exchange, and so we draw, less and less, on the arduous process of subjectivity to establish what we like and want.

The fashionability of an object prescribes its social meaning, thereby relieving us of the discursive problem of analysing and evaluating it. The effect of fashion is to make the individual reliant upon fashion as a short-hand script which expedites a great variety of social relations. If it has the unfortunate consequence of enshrining and constraining the everyday to a surface life where appearances and styles of performance are mistakenly or knowingly accepted as expressions of complex sensibilities, then it is a cost that is thought to be worthwhile. Fashionability may prevent the individual from encountering his or her own times, it may well be a disguised attack on human reflection, but it eases the fleeting encounters of the everyday and makes unnecessary an arduous or prolonged study of the character of the other. For these latter reasons, it is tacitly understood as useful.

The tragedy of modern social life is that individual character is corrupted by the kinds of sociality such as fashionability, which are commonly valued. Simmel maintained that the demands of modern city life made it necessary to simplify human exchange so that the individual could successfully enjoy daily exchanges with a multiplicity of others. While this codified manner of sociation, with its limited expression of sensibilities, has helped the individual in the immediate demands of everyday human commerce, there are long-term costs, such as its strangulation of the complex and varied aspects of human conduct which might otherwise emerge through less formulaic styles of social exchange. In its capacity as a common language, fashion may allow for sociality across a broad diversity of people, but it also means that everyday sociality comes to be dominated by the more diluted and undemanding properties of human exchange. In short, where there is a conflict between the subjectivity of the individual and the demands of public life, between the potentiality of sociality and what, indeed, transpires in the everyday, then we encounter what Simmel aptly called the modern tragedy.

In fashion we have an illustration of an enduring sociological problematic, namely, that of the tension between the individual's desire for individuality, and the demands for the regulation of that individuality in order to permit general sociation. The dynamic of fashion rests upon the individual's sense of an absence in him or herself of some desired commodity or capacity which needs to be obtained and satisfied. Thus, in following fashions, individuals consider they are doing their best to improve themselves. However, the nature of fashion, most particularly its constant flux, means that when the individual does attain the desired state of being, a sense of satisfaction does not remain for long: soon dissatisfaction once again impels the individual to seek a further object of fancy and, inevitably, all desires are in a state of melting away and being reformulated as ever new, but ever the same. The tragedy of fashion is that in its pursuit, irrespective of whether it is in the form of clothing, entertainment, ideas, popular practices or people, the individual has accepted a pre-figured system of meaning, a substitute for those interior discourses and experiences of sociation from which more engaged and complex meaning is possible.

Fashion, with its continual production of the new, and its corollary dismissal of all else, emphasizes a manner of sociality that must be relatively disengaged in order to allow movement on to the next style. The fashion *habitué* will become well practised in the reading of the fragmentary and fleeting; s/he will pare down the human character to its signs, namely, the outer garments and the choreography of the body. Nonetheless, fashionability, and the sense of order that it brings, is fleeting; even when we are in full fashion, we know that new and alternative fashions are imminent and, again, we will soon be in the shadows of the fashion colossus and silently impelled toward further changes in appearance.

By its capacity to create a sense of social order, fashion has the ability to act as a substantive barrier to the examined life. As Simmel has pointed out, the demands of a life passed in the cacophony of the metropolis, produces a desire for the prosaic, habitual and predictable in social relations. Fashionability does this by publicizing what is acceptable and desirable. The unacknowledged effect is to threaten the inner life with formulaic manners of acting and styles of appearing. While the tacit promise of fashionability may be to enlarge the self, to make more of the person, in actuality, it is also the mechanism by which human character is reduced and undermined by being confined to a surface existence.

The common idea of fashion as the harbinger of the new is, itself, a marketing strategy. Kennedy Fraser has succinctly described the view as a deception: 'fashion looks mobile and rebellious' but it is not – it is about consolidating the 'established centers of power' (1981:146). Bürger (1986) and Poggioli (1968) have added emphasis to the view by distinguishing fashion from the rebellious and socially disruptive avant-garde. The fashion *habitué* is deeply entrenched in the ordinary and tangible. Fashion makes sense to a great many people in a very short amount of time; it appears always to be logical, as if it were the inevitable next step, and its value derives from its being immediately intelligible to the many. Fashion always seems to be a direction that has to be taken, and its democratic appeal is that of being a legitimation of the already understood, that is, the present.

Fraser (1981) and others (Packard 1959; Molloy 1975; Davis 1985) have maintained that fashion and styles in appearance have the effect of making visible and concrete our personal circumstances; they are, in large part, physical representations of our economic position and location in the occupational hierarchy, and our competence with institutionalized modes of decorum. Styles of clothing signify fundamental statuses of gender, age and class which, in turn, provide a basis for social

5 Fashionability

engagement. It is a cliché to claim that styles in appearance are related to the public management of the body, that, in many ways, appearance prescribes the manners of exchange fundamental to everyday sociation. For instance, the professional, when clad in his or her business suit, knows the manners of exchange which would be *de rigueur* for that particular situation.

As well as directing certain styles of social engagement, fashion has the capacity to carry inherent contradictions. Some fashions assemble together concatenations of improbable characteristics; for example, the individual absorbed by the latest paraphernalia can appear to be, simultaneously, sexually suggestive and puritanical, demure and modest yet calculating and aggressive. In the case of Ralph Lauren casuals, the individual has paid a great deal of money not to look wealthy. Fashion advertisements, such as those for Calvin Klein and Gloria Vanderbilt jeans, combine similarly contradictory images. Advertising images promise the improbable: the image of a wantonly sexual yet pre-pubescent Brooke Shields in the Calvin Klein advertisements and the rejuvenated society matron of the Gloria Vanderbilt advertisements make little sense (Williamson 1983; Betterton 1987:40–69). They assume the probability of a roué residing in a child's body, and a free spirit being released from the body of the solid citizen. The images of fashion seem to stretch the imagination and make possible the integration of contradictory psychological properties, without revealing that these are fictions and devices which further the cult of individualism that characterizes the authenticating narrative of our time. Fashionability produces a sense of self which is contingent, always in flux, an image that floats on the surface of life, that is constituted from a multiplicity of unconnected moments. This parallels the ideals of self-production expressed in our cultural narratives.

Fraser has emphatically argued that fashions significantly define the modern culture, giving it a materialistic creed that 'holds that appearances are of greater significance than substance'. 'Fashion is a distorted imitation of life . . .' concerned, virtually by definition, with surfaces, images, appearances (Fraser 1981:145–8). These observations are important because

151

they suggest that even though we lack the convenience of, say, sumptuary laws to portray the social value of the individual, nonetheless we think we are still able to evaluate individuals by their appearance. However, when this occurs, when fashions shape human appearance to coincide with what we expect, then the idea must be recognized that fashions can act against the individual, and be mechanisms of social betrayal and interpersonal deceit. Fashions encourage us to view physical appearance as a means of judging one another, but when we do so, we substitute the process of excavating character with the readily available image of appearance. Our choice to be fashionable is also an agreement to accept the substitution of character with a series of images.

Fraser has maintained that in the twentieth century, we wrongly assume that 'clothing, furniture, and possessions of all kinds are, or ought to be, a form of self-expression' (1981:152). Fashion, she has declared, is in the business of deceiving us; its purpose is to 'trick outsiders into being impressed' with how we look and what we own (1981:154). Where the individual has been convinced that a pair of expensive shoes, knowledge of exotic cuisine, possession of exclusive art works and so on are reasonable means for expressing the self, then fashion has become a substitute for character.

The employment of fashions and styles in customs and appearance as abbreviations of human character is an attempt to ease human exchange by avoiding the difficulty of studying the other's intentions and capacities. Although we may know, at some chthonic level, that using the paraphernalia of appearance as a system of communication is misleading, the realization is continually overlaid and concealed by the edicts of the fashion industries. The fashion industries manage this by a 'skillful manipulation of people's urge to think that they are buying things for personal reasons' (Fraser 1981:259). The character of modern social life is defined, in part, by the fashion industries which manage to transform 'life's most precious and fragile assets into marketable products of transient worth' (1981:159).

Part III
The Fashioned Self

6

The Trial of Character

The importance attached to the idea of self is not a singularly modern preoccupation, although the advent of the consumer society has had a significant impact on the value placed upon self-identity. How we speak of personal identity and what we mean when referring to the self has been distinctly affected in the modern era, and while it is difficult to link precisely the social value accorded the self with any specific epoch, the modern era seems unique in the sovereignty it has granted the self.

Trilling (1972) and Elias (1978) independently designate the sixteenth century as the origins of the modern conceptualization of the self. Sennett (1976) sets the time somewhat later. However, historically locating changes in human consciousness is virtually impossible. Elias has rightly made the point that changes in human consciousness are so slow and so amorphous that they are almost imperceptible. Nonetheless, a common point of agreement seems to be that the emergence of the psychologistic individual designates the hallmark of modernity. This type of individual appears when the playing out of roles and the donning of social masks has come to be considered the best way of both engaging others and satisfying one's private desires. Unlike previous generations, the modern individual now shows a marked sense of self-consciousness as well as a

155

degree of anxiety over how s/he performs in public and what opinions others might frame of him or her.

Our current ideas of self and identity are not necessarily the culmination of an historical evolution, say, from the physiognomic theories of character, through a period of cultivated or fashioned identity to the contemporary conceptualization of the contingent self. There is no definite trajectory nor a developmental history of the self that can be convincingly mapped and annotated. The sense is more that certain ideas of self and patterns of social conduct have emerged at particular times as part of the tacit practical knowledge we have about ourselves, about others and how best to conduct our social affairs. So, it is not that the physiognomic principles gave way to ideas of the fashioned self which, in turn, have been diffused into a theory of contingency. On the contrary, these ideas persevere into the present and exist simultaneously with other explanations, in layered, sometimes contradictory assumptions. They constitute the narrative we employ to authenticate our understanding; for example, in reading human character, we draw simultaneously upon physiognomic features as well as the cultivated appearance of a particular persona. We employ an unsystematic body of knowledge about self and human character in our daily commerce. To understand why our conceptualization of character should be so inchoate in an era where the idea of the self is such a part of the everyday, requires us to put the idea of character on trial, as it were, to see what it has produced in terms of the nature of social relations.

In the late twentieth century, our understanding of the nature of human character seems to be derived from a motley assemblage of contradictory ideas. It would be reasonable to conclude from this striation of assumptions that questions about the nature of character are not a vital and working part of our everyday discourse. That we hastily read character physiognomically, knowing all the while that the other may have had a face lift, or be wearing coloured contact lenses, or have had a hair transplant or be using hair dye, infers that we are less interested in knowing character than the value we place upon it would suggest. We know that appearances can be created and that dressing in a particular fashion will most certainly convey to others a more or less predictable impression. Our understanding of identity is so closely interwoven with ideas and assumptions which run in parallel with each other, or in contradiction, or make sense only as strategies to help order our everyday interactions, that it seems reasonable to conclude that our knowledge of human character and our speculations about the nature of our own consciousness and that of others are remarkably incoherent and unsystematized.

It is a conclusion that Elias (1978) would endorse in his study of the civilizing process. In his observations that we lack an understanding of the meaning of social progress, that we are reticent in accepting responsibility for the conditions of modern society and that we are incoherent in our assertions about what would make a society civilized, progressive and humanitarian, he is also inferring that we hold confused theories about human character and the nature of the social world we inhabit. It is the argument of this present work that while we may live in a social milieu which continuously places value upon self-knowledge, self-feeling, self-development, self-actualization, self-control, self-indulgence and self-promotion, we are simultaneously underdeveloped in our understanding of the nature of self. The concept of self may be a salient feature of our everyday conduct, but an elaborated understanding of what it means to have character, what the relationship is between the individual and the historical structure of a society, remains much neglected.

Elias (1978) has nominated the sixteenth century as the clearest point from which to date the emergence of those salient features which typify modern identity. It is a point of reference shared, in large part, by many others (see Huizinga 1952; Barbu 1960; Ariès 1962; Trilling 1972; Braudel 1981; Duby 1988a). Elias has argued that from the sixteenth century, the perspective developed that not only were outward physical appearances representative of inner character but that the individual's gestures and manners could also be treated as elongations of the inner world of mental and emotional dispositions (Elias 1978:56). Elias has shown that the early manuals and compendia of manners which instructed individuals on table

157

III *The Fashioned Self*

habits, bedroom manners, deportment and so on were also newly composed instructions to the individual to take cognizance of others in ways that had not been previously observed. These instructions were not a refutation of the physiognomic perspective; indeed, it was still believed that much of the individual's character was evident in his or her physical attributes. These new rules of social intercourse were reflective of the changes introduced to society by alterations in economic and political structures.

Ariès (1962), Trilling (1972) and Braudel (1981) have each noted that alterations in human consciousness, which finally culminate in the modern psychologistic individual, can be seen reflected in changes to the physical environment of social life, beginning from the sixteenth-century. Braudel (1981:283–308; see also Girouard 1980), for example, has recognized the changes to the spatial order of housing, such as the differentiation of rooms by function into a bedroom, dining room, a closet for privacy, and other innovations, such as the restyling of furniture and the remaking of the long bench into a single-seater chair, as being reflective of changes in ideas about the comfort and needs of the individual; these, in turn, suggested that shifts were occurring in the understanding of self. When Trilling (1972:24) suggested that 'it is when he (*sic*) becomes an individual that a man lives more and more in private rooms', he could well have been speaking in support of Braudel's assertion that changes in personal temperament have long been visible in the physical dimensions of the individual's life, in the different ways people begin to express an interest in personal comforts, luxury, privacy, fashionability and so on. Thus, when personal possessions such as clothes become subject to fashions and function as insignia of self-adornment, when areas of a house are separated from each other and designated with specific functions, when eating practices are altered by the introduction of table manners and the individuation of place settings, then it would seem that the individual is beginning to act in ways that express a concern for how others see him or her and how s/he wishes, in turn, to be seen by those others.

The expansion of trade, and its accompanying flow of ideas, had an important influence on the sixteenth-century European world. As Braudel (1981; 1982) has described in fascinating detail, the wheels of commerce brought changes to the individual's everyday world. New goods introduced by foreigners and traders generated new ideas. Braudel has argued that entrepreneurial trade was a major factor in producing an altered perspective on the society and the individual. Elias (1978; 1982) has similarly argued that the modernist perspective begins at this time arising from alterations in human exchange and the demands thus generated. As individuals come to meet with others who are different from themselves, a degree of self-consciousness develops which gives individuals a sense that they are separate and distinct from others. In so doing, individuals develop the ability to think about and against the customs of the day (Elias 1978:251). It is also from these ideas that Elias sees the growing legitimacy of the characterization of the individual as *homo clausus*. It is this understanding of identity which sharply distinguishes the modern personality and it is also this conceptualization which, Elias has argued, produces a misunderstanding of the relationship between personal identity and the nature of the social order.

> The conception of the individual as *homo clausus*, a little world in himself who ultimately exists quite independently of the great world outside, determines the image of man in general. Every other human being is likewise seen as a *homo clausus*; his core, his being, his true self appears likewise as something divided within him by an invisible wall from everything outside, including every other human being. (1978:249)

It is a view which has endured into contemporary times, so that now it is common to say that people have a self, a core of true identity that is somehow locked away inside them, severed from all other people who are outside. Elias (1978:245–8) has argued that this split into the separate concepts of the individual and the society is misleading; 'there is no structural feature of man that justifies our calling one thing the core of man and another the shell' (1978:259). There is, in short, no structure of self but only a manner of representing and addressing oneself which reflects upon the nature of the particular

159

social circumstances in which it occurs. Whilst the nomenclature of the self may designate the existence of a realm separate from the social, this does not grant the self an ontology. Elias makes the further point (which is both a conclusion of this present study into the fashioned self, and a prelude to the argument I wish to outline in this chapter) that as long as we cling to the idea of *homo clausus*, to the idea of an individuated, unique and precious self, the civilizing possibilities of human society will be constrained (Elias 1978:263). Maintaining the view of the *homo clausus* means that our understanding of personal identity is mythic and like other myths of the day, as Barthes (1973) has shown us, it functions to impede our interest in more detailed analyses.

Trilling (1972) has been exact in nominating the precipitating conditions of the new psychological perspective. He has acknowledged that the idea of self-consciousness has been, to some extent, a commonplace truth throughout Western civilization. We have always had social mechanisms by which individuals could designate themselves as separable entities. Indeed, the ancient Delphic and Greek injunction to 'know thyself' contains within it various allusions to the individual's capacity for self-consciousness. To know oneself also infers that one does not know oneself or that one is assuming postures that are not true to oneself, perhaps adopting such poses for the purpose of deceiving others. In short, the glosses and permutations with which we, in the late twentieth century, garner the idea of the self could reasonably be read into the ancient phrase. However, Trilling takes the sixteenth-century inscription, *Totus mundus facit histrionem*, inscribed at Shakespeare's Globe Theatre, as recording a significant shift in the characterization of the individual and the social world.[1] The phrase (in idiomatic Latin) translates as 'the world makes the actor.' This can be interpreted as meaning that the nature of social life is such that we are compelled to develop an ability to act; it can also mean that acting is not a skill to be taught but emerges from the richness of the individual's life. This would

---

[1] Adams (1961:31–2) has reported the inscription to be *Totus mundus agit histrionem* on the sign hanging over the door of the Globe.

mean that the more worldly the individual, the more capable s/he will be of acting, pretending, posing, even deceiving. The phrase cannot be literally translated to mean that everyone tells lies, but it is worth considering that in the light of a wider exploration of how modern consciousness has been formed, such an interpretation is not impossible. This phrase, immortalized at the Globe, seemed to Trilling to advertise the performative nature and theatricality of social life, and to suggest that a shift of consciousness was taking place, at the time, about the nature of the self and what meaning could be extracted from the ancient instruction to know thyself.

Trilling regarded this inscription as heralding the psychologistic individual because it characterized human exchange as legitimately proceeding along several planes of interpretation simultaneously: one could act uncharacteristically, one could disguise oneself and one could pretend to be someone else. The modern individual then became recognizable as an accumulation of roles, and character became, in turn, a striation of performances. Trilling's characterization of sixteenth-century England as being a society 'preoccupied to an extreme degree with dissimulation, feigning and pretense' (Trilling 1972:13) was based on the popularity of the theatres. The Globe (1598) and the Fortune (1600) commonly held audiences of over a thousand people (Laslett in Trilling 1972:21), and in them people were seeing life represented as a plethora of mistaken identities, subterfuges and mysteries, where lovers were impersonated, the improbable seemed more common than the ordinary, and the customs of the everyday were constantly breached by the imagination. In the theatrical world where all was pretence, and even the female roles were played by boys, the characters were rarely what they seemed.

To pretend to be someone else meant that the products of one's imagination could alter one's social universe. The popular theatre showed individuals that their own capacity to act out roles was a natural attribute of the human condition. Learning to act, to dissemble, to lie as a part of one's everyday conduct, endowed the individual with another dimension. Thus, an inner realm of preoccupation was carved out in which the individual could enjoy a sense of 'internal space' and imagine

161

him- or herself differently, say, as an object of interest to others or as a stranger who might be standing outside the moment looking on (Trilling 1972:24). The sixteenth-century individual began to rethink the world and entertain the heretical idea that one could socialize with guile and perpetrate ploys and acts of cunning upon others who would be tricked and manipulated for one's own amusement and gain.

The effect of this new dramaturgy of thinking was to forge a psychological perspective. Individuals recognized the existence of an inner dimension which allowed them to reflect and feel in ways that were convoluted, complex and contrary to expectation. By recognizing that one's thoughts and imagination were the hidden, invisible dimensions of everyday life, individuals encountered the forces of desire and playfulness; the world became a domain separate from themselves in which they could take deliberate actions in order to bring about desired ends. Shakespeare's plays are among the earliest examples of this particularly modern sense of individuality. Previously, drama had presented typical behaviours; characters were identified as personifications of universal vices and virtues, or as embodiments of one of the four humours or temperaments. But, with Shakespeare, characters became internally richer; for example, the character of Hamlet can be seen to possess a variety of mood, desire, talent and capacity. With the arrival of the unique individual who could embody various personae simultaneously, and with the recognition of an external world in which these facets of character could be played out, the shape of society became more complex and varied.

The eighteenth-century Venetian Giambattista Vico contributed in another way to the aggrandizement of the concept of self in Western civilization. He argued that human nature was distinguished by the ability to objectify and categorize a world unattached to the individual, thereby allowing individuals to make sense of that which was not their own. Vico's ruminations on human nature and social life gave recognition to the importance of self-consciousness. His 'new science' established the study of human consciousness as fundamental to any understanding of the objective world. Berlin (1969:374–5) has described Vico's contribution as having 'uncovered a sense of knowing which is basic to all human studies'. By nominating the sense of knowing as fundamental to an understanding of the world, the Vichian perspective placed the concept of self at the heart of any intellectual enterprise.

Having argued for the value of the self, Vico then proceeded to show how confounding it could be. He maintained that 'only with great difficulty does (the human mind) come to understand itself by means of reflection' (Vico 1744, paragraph 236). More often than not, we do not reflect on the world in such a way that its mysteries are revealed to us; our self-consciousness intrudes and becomes a source of distortion because, 'when men are ignorant of the natural causes producing things, and they cannot explain them by analogy with similar things, they attribute their own nature to them ... the human mind ... makes itself the rule of the universe' (Vico 1744, paragraph 180). Vico thought we too readily assumed that our knowledge was true, that our views were self-evident and 'as old as the world', when, indeed, they were not so. The majesty we accorded our own perceptions made the self into a barrier to understanding. Vico came to this conclusion because 'whenever men can form no idea of distant and unknown things, they judge them by what is familiar and at hand' (Vico 1744, paragraph 181). To Vico such solipsism spoke of human ignorance because only ignorant people know everything and make themselves the measure of all; it is the learned who live with doubt and contradiction. Elias's condemnation of the modern individual, the *homo clausus*, who has misconceived the nature of the external world and thereby misconceived his or her own place in it, draws implicitly on the legacies of the Vichian perspective.

Sennett's (1976) historical analysis of the distinctive character of the modern individual rests upon the unique experiences generated by the growing cosmopolitanism of the West and a life increasingly passed amongst strangers. In the flourishing public life of the eighteenth-century city, he has described how the formality of interpersonal exchange signified that an ability to act, to pretend to be what one was not, to conceal oneself behind a performance, was regarded as a natural feature of sociality (Sennett 1976:3); 'manners and ritual interchanges with strangers are looked on as at best formal and dry, at worst as phony. The stranger himself is a threatening figure, and few people can take pleasure in the world of strangers, the cosmopolitan city.'

In the public domain, in a life amongst strangers, the manner of sociality became regulated by customs and rituals which were informed by certain physiognomic assumptions. Character was regarded as an inherent quality of one's existence, which meant that the individual was in possession of an interior world of private emotions, sentiments and proclivities which could presumably be disclosed at any time, whether one wished it or not. One could not be confident of knowing who the stranger was that one encountered in the public domain, so one needed to be sure not to reveal too much of one's self to them; this was achieved by regulating one's outward appearance and manner of acting. Exerting this kind of self-control produced a sense of detachment from any inward, private feelings and sentiments. Importantly, the individual became more conscious of a need to keep separate a private inner realm of feelings and this, in turn, ensured that disruptions to sociality from the inadvertent disclosure of any of these private feelings were held in check. The undergirding assumption was that human nature could be a dangerous and mysterious force which could not always be socially accommodated. When it was unleashed unexpectedly it could disturb the contours of the society (Sennett 1976:338).

A consequence of this dual conceptualization of self and society is that when a private realm of interiority becomes so cherished and protected from external influences, it can be seen to atrophy. This is the argument of Sennett's historical account of the empty modern self. Other influences have also been of importance. Increased commerce and industrialization altered the topography of society and its system of social stratification, and in so doing, rearranged the architecture of the self. In a society newly divided between the commercial and domestic, between public and private, where social mobility became possible and the financial status of the individual could fluctuate according to circumstance and serendipity, the idea of a deterministic human character became much less convincing. As Sennett has noted:

> Men came to believe they were the authors of their own characters, that every event in their lives must have a meaning in terms of defining themselves, but what this meaning was, the instabilities and contradictions of their lives made it difficult to say ... Gradually this mysterious, dangerous force which was the self came to define social relations. It became a social principle. (1976:339)

When new social arrangements came into being, individuals began to think of themselves as capable of shaping their own characters in the same way that they were capable of shaping their social and economic destiny. This new fashion in thinking marked the 'coming of age' of the modern contingent self. In the fluid world of the nineteenth century, in an environment of burgeoning capitalism, enterprise and mechanical invention, those individuals with acumen and ambition seemed able to change their social stations and fortunes. By the exploitation of certain personal attributes they could accrue wealth, power, status and privilege. For those who could remake their social and economic world, the remaking of the self seemed equally possible and, indeed, this was the next logical step. In a society of material abundance and fashionability, where being in public always required a performance of sorts, the individual learned to act, and, often, to pretend to be what s/he was not. The less rigid stratification of the commercial nineteenth century required of the individual who sought to pursue social and commercial opportunities, a much greater degree of self-scrutiny and self-consciousness. Using fashionable items and commodities as devices for claiming a particular character or personal identity became an increasingly common ploy. Thus, the practices of presenting character and fashioning or styling a public persona became more common.

The creation of wealth and the production of material commodities fuelled a belief that society could be shaped by technical expertise to suit one's purposes. The expansion of technology and the application of the mechanical principle impinged upon human consciousness to make it seem as if personal qualities and skills could be fashioned or obtained in much the same manner as material commodities. Marx had presciently threaded the idea into the social fabric that the individual's desire to accumulate goods and power, and to identify human attributes from the possession of material goods, was a misunderstanding of human character. It produced a jaundiced view of the value of human labour and it invested the material object, the product of the individual's labour, with fanciful characteristics and capacities. The consumer ethic produced a commodified individual and a fetishized object. A century later, the equation of material ownership with taste and of physical appearance with human character had endured strongly enough for Marcuse to note derisively that 'people recognize themselves in their commodities; they find their soul in their automobile, hi-fi set, split-level home, kitchen equipment' (1964:24).

This conflation of personal identity with material objects and the investiture of personal character into objects signal an increasing confusion in the discourses surrounding the nature of personal identity and human character. How can individuals find the essentials of their character in the objects which they know to have been manufactured by others? What unique value can an individual possess when it is the ownership of goods and the wielding of power which hold the greatest status in modern society? In the development of human consciousness, when we come to think of ourselves as an objective entity with an interior reservoir of largely unexplicated ideas, beliefs, attitudes and desires, we arrive at the perspective of the *homo clausus*. As we begin to think of ourselves as a separable entity, we also think of the society as an entity with its own character. Thus, the modern individual, the *homo clausus*, is born contiguously with the ability to think of the world as separate and conquerable. As the society is seen to have a life of its own, with laws and functions which make it seem orderly and natural, so the individual is cast as a separate entity who is sometimes part of the society, and at other times, in opposition to it.

6 The Trial of Character

The relationship between the individual and the society is rich in cultural assumptions about the nature of the human self. Turner (1976:989–1007) has argued that, in contemporary society, it has become common to look for sources of personal identity through institutional membership. Often the individual's private discovery of self is made through immersion in an institutional framework such as marriage, the church, a profession. However, Turner goes on to say that when institutions become disorderly, corrupt, impersonal or hostile, then the individual cannot extract a stable sense of identity or feel anchored in the society. The dissident writer George Konrad has taken this characterization of the alienated individual as typifying the modern individual. In his novel *The Case Worker*, he has vividly described the modern individual as a product of the rationalized state, the bureaucratic colossus. The nature of everyday life in the modern society is such that it produces an individual who is relentlessly petty and self-serving. In *The Case Worker*, Konrad's protagonist is a civil servant, a thoroughly mainstream member of society, who imagines himself immune to the social forces which bring about the despair of his clients. It is an obvious irony that the protagonist is a social worker or counsellor, a professional factotum of the state's therapeutic services, who cannot help himself, yet feels charged with the responsibility of helping others.

Konrad presents his fictive bureaucrat as disdainful of his clients; he thinks them too susceptible to the influences and degradations of their circumstances. He is scornful because they respond too readily to external factors, as if they were chameleons taking on the qualities of their environs; 'every institution makes for a specific state of mind. At the circus my client laughs, at the public baths he dreams, on the streetcar he stares into space, at a boxing match he is aggressive, in the cemetery subdued, and so on' (Konrad 1975:14–15). This also applies to the case worker, the archetype of the modern individual.

(I) feel sorry for him (the modern individual) because so many obstacles have impeded his development. It would be commendable if his relations with his environment were somewhat more complex, if the rules he chose to live by were a little less conventional. But his system is depressingly lacking in complexity, his income wretched, his physical surroundings dreary, his vision blurred, his burden heavy. (Konrad 1975:16)

Fashioning an identity from an environment which is itself constraining, even subversive of human ideals, produces an equally hollow resonance in the individual. The technical and economic conditions conducive to the development of a highly industrialized society also act upon the consciousness of the individual. Konrad's modern bureaucrat, who is the pivot of the bourgeois social and economic order is, lamentably, a *character redux*. He is a character who thinks of himself as fortunate, with opportunities different from those of the other members of society but, at the same time, this character acts unwittingly against his own better interests. A *character redux* accepts circumstances as if they were fortifying, without fully apprehending that they may also be his or her undoing. A *character redux* treats cultural traits and values as if they were second nature to him or her without recognizing them as anomalies and points of alienation. For example, Konrad has described the successful member of bourgeois society as self-seeking and mean-spirited. In the instance of the case worker, he has gained a privileged, or at least, secure position by being competitive, ambitious and opportunistic. Such attributes are accepted as prerequisites for the attainment of social success. At the same time, this attainment has been accompanied by acts and sentiments hostile to any ideals of social progress; thus, the modern bourgeois shows a discernible loss of civility to others, an increased intolerance toward those who do not validate his or her particular achievements, and a failure to recognize the accidental and contingent nature of his or her own success. Simmel has suggested much the same in *The Philosophy of Money* (1980) where he has argued that a society dominated by money, power and status produces a form of human sociality which inevitably becomes artificial and repressive. Konrad's fictive character could be Simmel's bourgeois; he has become mean-spirited with his successes and increased status.

6 The Trial of Character

When I have change in my pocket, I tend to cross the street
when I see a beggar; I hate visiting sick people in hospital; I
grumble when I have to stand up for an old lady on the bus;
rather than listen to the snivelling of the widower next door, I
avoid saying good morning to him. (Konrad 1975:21)

In Konrad's fictive world the measures of progress and civility have become largely indecipherable. The individual lives
without knowing whether his or her horizons are narrow, or
whether society could be better. The basis for making judge-
ments about one's private principles as well as public morality
seems undefinable. For an individual to take an interest in
moral questions, s/he must have a sense of power and a belief
in the possibility of bringing about social change. Where there
is no such sense of power, these questions remain derelict. Elias
has made the same point with his description of our contemporary loss of a sense of progress. In the modern era, we no
longer speak much of making progress, even though our technical accomplishments have been far greater than those of
previous epochs. Elias contends that we no longer do so because we have lost the moral foundations upon which to judge
what is and what is not progress, what is and what is not
humanly valuable. As he has stated:

> In the preceding centuries, in which actual progress was already
> very palpable yet still slow and relatively limited, the idea of
> further, future progress had the character of an ideal toward
> which its adherents were striving and which possessed high
> value precisely as an ideal. In the twentieth century, when
> actual progress in science, technology, health, the standard of
> living and not least in the reduction of inequality between
> people exceeds by far, in the older industrial nations, the prog-
> ress in all previous centuries, progress has ceased for many
> people to be an ideal. The voices of those who doubt all this
> actual progress are growing more numerous. (Elias 1987:237)

It is a contradiction to claim that the individual has the
capacity for both autonomous action and the expression of
authentic desires when, at the very same time, the character
and nature of the social order in which s/he lives remains

169

incomprehensible and intractable to him or her. There cannot be a valid sense of individuality when the balance between the individual and the social world is not understood. After all, the claim of individuality is also a political claim. Thus, we cannot portray ourselves as having a strong sense of self, when, at the same time, we have little understanding of how a society is possible, or how it is best organized. Without a developed discourse on the nature of the social experience, we may be fashioning ourselves in accord with shifting institutional interests, some of which may embody a latent social ethic subtly opposed to our better interests.

We live in an age dominated by an emphasis on individualism. Liberty and equality are widely accepted as essential freedoms, and civil rights are taken for granted as the prerogative of independent and autonomous beings. Yet, the point can be inferred from Veblen, Simmel, Elias, Konrad and others, that the individual cannot claim self-knowledge unless s/he also understands and controls the character of the social universe in which s/he lives. So, to lionize individualism without a complementary emphasis upon social and political discourse can have the contrary effect, namely, that of undermining the constituents from which human character is developed. That is, when our self-interests become stronger than our communal sense, and when our social relations become skewed by a relentless search for novel amusements, then the idea of individuality becomes an instrument that obscures the authentic nature of personal identity. Whilst it is now a commonplace to be fervent about our civil rights, to demand this opportunity and that privilege on the basis of a lionized individualism, it is rarely recognized that these demands, when directed towards failed institutions (as Konrad has described), have the unintended consequence of more deeply obfuscating the nature of the human self. Our demands for this social privilege or that public service, as if they were rights of existence, prevent our understanding that the origins of self-identity reside in a mutualism between the individual's everyday sphere of existence and the transcendental ideals of social progress (see Heller 1985). Thus, the paradox of contemporary individualism is that the individual cannot assume full stature when that stature is wrought by a withering away of a sense of community; an individual cannot ascend above the community without becoming dessicated and, by the same token, a society cannot colonize the lifeworld of the individual without destroying it. So, the inherent contradiction of the claim that selfhood has a high cultural value in modern society becomes glaringly obvious when we recognize how dominant are those social imperatives (such as fashions, self-promotion, the cult of the body) which undercut and even prevent our realization of the nature of the societal experience.

The outpouring of creativity which accompanied the defining of the self in the Renaissance has not been carried through to the modern era. The outpouring of attention on to the modern self has not produced an unequivocally creative and progressive discourse addressed to contemporary social problems. Indeed, the opposite could be argued; the intense focus on the modern self has diverted attention away from the practices of critique. In the late twentieth century, when the impetus for conspicuous consumption and the commodification of all manner of objects and entertainments seems near its zenith, the self has become, as well, a marketable entity. When we recognize how centrally important the contemporary self has become in the consumer marketplace, how much the idea of personal identity has been commodified by industries in the business of producing adjuncts to the self, it can be seen how the self has been greatly diminished.

The idea of self may occupy a central place in our everyday practices, but this is no assurance of its substantiality. On the contrary, the new fashioned self appears more like a concatenation of disparate elements than it does a coherent manner of living in and understanding the world. The intellectuality and creativity of the Renaissance self has not been replicated in the contemporary explosion of interest in the self. It is as if the idea of self has been on trial, and after four hundred years, it has been found less than its promise and, finally, an impediment. Individuals have been dwarfed by the social system, by the twin colossus of bureaucracy and industry, and, more poignantly, by their own impossible desires and compulsions which drive them to fashion themselves in iconic imitation of

171

the successful, powerful, rich, famous, beautiful, youthful and talented. Such is the modern world where the excitation of the nerves and the compulsive search for amusement propel individuals to pursue the fashionable and fleeting, and in so doing, neglect to examine the social conditions in which they find themselves. It is a Simmelian world in which the cacophony of the metropolis has deafened the individual, a world which Steiner (1981) has claimed can only be understood from the margins, when the individual has been degraded or expelled from the mainstream because of a failure to meet the norms, in instances, say, of bankruptcy, mental illness, physical disability, juridical enquiry and so on. The modern individual is a *character redux* who lives in a world where everything flows and nothing abides, where all gives way and nothing is fixed, where the living are doomed but few know it. The modern self has become like other perishables, 'cut down to size, packaged in plastic, and offered for consumption complete with instructions for preparation and a sell-by date' (Boyne 1988:542).

Subsequently, in the modern era, we must contemplate the idea that the self has become a disintegrative element (Morgenthau and Person 1978:339). The modern self takes its shape from fashion and not from a critique of the times. The fashioned self is continually produced and renewed. The individual is continually instructed to respond to desires which, under the aegis of fashion, are ever-shifting. The versatility and responsiveness of the modern self have produced a surfeit of identities. The self has become a mass-produced, market product; buy this in order to be that. The self has been transposed into an icon and a fetish; it is simultaneously a display of conspicuous consumption and a commodity with an artifical value.

Self-identity has become a product which can be purchased from a marketplace of ideas and images produced by a generation of culture industries. This is the paradox of modernity, namely, that the self is fashioned from external, often purchasable elements rather than wrought from the private ruminations of an individual. Identity and character have become elements of the public culture which has itself been absorbed into one's consciousness without reflection. The origins of self in the examined life have been bypassed; character, forged from the private experience of an internal universe, where moral positions, ideas concerning human progress and codes of ideal conduct are evaluated over time, seems to have been superseded. The rumination of the examined life has become, instead, a traumatic experience, a form of mental disarray and, thus, to be avoided. The final result is that dedication to self-development and self-presentation produces a corollary of insidious political and social quietism. It would seem, then, that in the process of shopping for a self, we have unwittingly bypassed its origins in the experience of subjectivity.

Arendt (1947:16) has argued that when privately experienced psychological effects are elevated in importance, when the individual can only estimate the value of all else by the way s/he feels, then an understanding of the social, of what humans are capable of, has been annihilated. The modern elevation of the self has allowed us to forget that the measure of an humane society is that all members recognize their moral obligations towards one another. When the recounting of one's own emotional responses has become the individual's instrument for reading social reality, then a sense of dissociation from any responsibility for the nature of social life has come to seem normal. At this point, Arendt has ironically indicated, we have arrived at 'the great privilege of being unburdened by care for the world' (1968:14).

The idea of the self which four centuries ago galvanized Western society, has become, in the modern era, a disintegrative element. Morgenthau and Person (1978) have nominated the late nineteenth century as an exact moment when a shift can be discerned in the character of self and its moral ties with society. Oscar Wilde has provided them with an example of a life lived according to a new definition of the world. He is portrayed as having made it seem possible to redefine the world in accord with one's self-interests and desires. The myth that surrounded the figure of Oscar Wilde proclaimed that individuality had finally attained its zenith; one could act as one wished, the world could be rewritten in one's own hand, there were no legitimate constraints preventing the expression of one's capacities. While Wilde's own experiences ultimately

173

illustrated the opposite to this (Ellmann 1988), in the context of the emergent modern self, the myth of Wilde's personal philosophy has been used as a signpost to the new era.

The modern individual has become highly literate in the language of the interaction ritual. We have wholeheartedly accepted as self-evidently true that appearances can reveal much about the individual, including those qualities of character which are internal and not immediately apparent. We have come to accept, readily enough, that dressing in a particular style will create a predictable impression: a man in a business suit and a woman in a dress are thought to be eloquent in their endorsement of gender as well as the economic and social status quo. Other icons of identity, such as lipstick, the necktie, high-heeled shoes, the moustache, are effectively employed as suggestions of identity. Modern individuals know how to fashion an appearance, just as Wilde is purported to have done with his velvet suit, abundant neckties and green carnation buttonhole. Similarly, it can be thought that donning a pair of horn-rimmed spectacles will effectively exude an aura of intellectuality, or wearing a business suit will suggest respectability and formality, or a *décolleté* dress will affirm femininity.

Of course, this is not so. Intellectuality is not a pair of horn-rimmed spectacles; such spectacles merely suggest a popular, immediately comprehensible image of the bookish individual. We know that these icons are employed to express certain styles of self, and it is understood that these signs do not guarantee the actuality of character. Foucault's (1983) discourse on image and reality, using Magritte's assertion that a painting of a pipe is not a pipe (*Ceci n'est pas une pipe*), shows the hiatus between the sign and the object. It may be obvious that a painted pipe cannot be used for smoking tobacco, and that horn-rimmed spectacles are not capable of bringing ideas into focus, but when we say that the wearer of these spectacles looks intellectual, or that the painting of a pipe is a pipe, we have repudiated the obvious. The images of the spectacles and the painting have been confused with the reality. After all, how can an image be the object or the idea that it represents? In the same way, how can a dress make a woman feminine? How can a necktie make a man serious or respectable or stylish?

174

This is the important idea that Oscar Wilde alluded to in his famous aphorism in *The Picture of Dorian Gray*: 'It is only shallow people who do not judge by appearances. The true mystery of the world is the visible, not the invisible' (Wilde 1966:32). It is the same idea that Foucault has pronounced as the characterizing feature of modern times, 'signs invoke the very thing of which they speak' (Foucault 1983:22).

In *The Picture of Dorian Gray*, Wilde has demonstrated how the obvious can be misread, indeed, is commonly misread. By successfully donning a mask, playing a role, constructing the artificial, the modern individual has come to think that his or her autonomy has been proved. It is as if the execution of these complex social gestures is a proof that the individual must have fully understood the mysteries of human engagement. Goffman's work implies much the same; the socially adroit individual is someone who plays the roles, meets expectations, executes the customs of the situation with aplomb. Such an individual, who is continuously acting out and fashioning a self identity, is regarded as having well understood the dynamics of human sociality (Goffman 1967).

This is the skew in the modern sensibility. Oscar Wilde was not his necktie; Dorian Gray was not his unchanging visage; the bespectacled individual is not necessarily the continuum of the image. We have come to read the signs, the obvious elements of the individual's persona, as if they were the constituents of what they represent. When Foucault stated that 'signs invoke the very thing of which they speak' (1983:22), and when Oscar Wilde wrote that 'the true mystery of the world is the visible, not the invisible' (1966:32), both meant that what we make of the obvious and what we extract from the visible, we mistakenly accept as the truth of the matter. That the modern individual is fashioned from a cultivated attention to detail reveals what we understand to be the nature of modern character. That the modern individual is fashioned and more interested in the authority of the sign than the elements it represents, reveals to us what we think is the nature of the modern self. The sign has been mistaken for its referent.

The historical failure of the idea of self stems from its central location in the modern experience. We have acquired the knack

175

of appraising the world through the signs of the self; as such we have failed to realize all the implications of the phrase, *totus mundus facit histrionem*. We have become actors and we have acquired the ability to dissemble but, we have not understood as well that the capacity to act is itself a representation of how we understand the workings of the world. That we see the modern self arising from our fashioning of an identity, tells us of our acceptance of our contingent nature. The fashioned, malleable self is an obvious representation of character. That we accept the obvious signs as if they were character itself reveals our failure to produce a self. The consequence of this confusion between the obvious and real is the hallmark of our times.

7

The Self as Sign

Oscar Wilde's nineteenth-century story *The Picture of Dorian Gray* is, in part, both an exposition and a repudiation of the view that character is immanent in appearance. The story shows how Dorian Gray, a spectacularly handsome man, used his beauty to conceal from others his self-indulgent and murderous capabilities. The obvious moral of the tale is that appearances must be read as appearances or else they mislead. The character Lord Henry Wotton pronounces, 'It is only shallow people who do not judge by appearances. The true mystery of the world is the visible, not the invisible' (Wilde 1966:32). The aphorism is arresting because it appears to contradict a self-evident truth, namely, that we should not be influenced by appearances, we should not judge a book by its cover. Yet, Lord Henry Wotton's pronouncement seemingly instructs us in the reverse – by all means judge by appearance, one is wrong not to, after all the mysteries of the world are in the visible.

In the world of Wilde's story, judging character by appearance seemed common enough; Wotton judged Dorian by his appearance, Dorian judged Sibyl Vane by hers and Sibyl reciprocated with Dorian. However, Wilde does not mean to leave the idea at that. He was also urging that we query the common belief that appearances are revealing. It can happen, after all, that we may find someone's appearance so arresting that we stifle any further efforts for a developed interchange with them. In time, the evidence of this mistake in judgement is revealed in the portrait of Dorian Gray, his hidden self, which becomes 'seared with the lines of suffering and thought', a 'visible emblem of conscience', and a 'mask of his shame' (Wilde 1966:78–81). Wilde has the portrait record Dorian's immoral conduct and in so doing allows Dorian's physical beauty to remain an untarnished disguise until his death. It is the portrait, the iconic and hidden self, which becomes blistered in appearance and is, thereby, truly revelatory of Dorian's character.

The Picture of Dorian Gray is a demonstration of the ease with which human appearance is used as a statement of character, which was, to Wilde, the real mystery of the world. Physical appearances cannot express human character, yet we think they do. At the same time, in a contrary vein, we like to think of human character as a private repository available to others only under the strictest conditions, such as religious confession, psychotherapeutic revelation or marital secrecy. It is not to be found at the surface, amongst the finicky details of social conventions and the rules of public conduct. Nonetheless, that we often deduce a view of the other's character from the details of his or her physical appearance, indicates that our understanding of human character is riddled with contradictions. We expect physical appearance to be revealing of character, and so we thoroughly fashion our appearances, but we also believe in an essential self not unlike that postulated by the physiognomists. In *The Picture of Dorian Gray*, Wilde has given voice to both these views. As if in full sympathy with the physiognomic view, Dorian said of his own portrait, 'it is the face of my soul' (Wilde 1966:117). His sin was capable of being written across his face. Indeed, 'if a wretched man has a vice, it shows itself in the lines of his mouth, the droop of his eyelids, the moulding of his hands even' (1966:117). In the story, of course, the personage of Dorian Gray shows none of these signs; that we can make sense of these conflicting views is, as Wilde has suggested, an enduring mystery of human conduct.

The sociological insight that can be extracted from Wilde's

7 The Self as Sign

story is that puzzling as the practice may appear, people do judge others on the spurious grounds of appearance. Goffman has accepted this as a fundamental of human sociality; for him, there is no question that appearance matters. He opened his work on stigma with a letter quoted from Nathanael West's fictional work *Miss Lonelyhearts* in which a young girl with a face deformed by the absence of a nose, laments her daily trials (Goffman 1963). In West's story, the young girl has written to the Miss Lonelyhearts column of a daily metropolitan newspaper to ask, 'what did I do to deserve such a terrible bad fate?' and 'ought I commit suicide?' She signed the letter 'Desperate' (West 1967). The poignancy of the fictive letter lies in the injustice of the young girl's despair. The contorted face has made her an outsider, a supernumerary, even though it has also heightened her capacity for subtle social analysis and reflection. The young girl is far too distressed by her appearance to recognize that it has engendered within her a more complex and interesting character. Her greater social skills remain an unrecognized reward which do not compensate for the visible facial oddity.

That appearance matters is a well-known, if covert, law of sociality. However, embedded in it are questions about the ways in which appearances matter and to whom. The obvious answer is that appearance matters because it is thought to affect how others regard us. Individuals considered to be attractive are granted other valued attributes. Social and behavioural psychologists have long evidenced this connection; some have also acknowledged its basic injustice. Nonetheless, this truism of human behaviour is broadly held; we are influenced by the appearance of others and, in turn, we ourselves are judged in similar fashion.

The professional commentators interviewed in the film of Daisy's face lift asserted unanimously that physical attractiveness had a great influence on the ebb and flow of everyday social exchange (Rubbo 1983). Most people, most of the time, judged others on the basis of physical appearance, even in those exacting situations like job interviews where it was commonly thought that talents and capacities were more important than an individual's physical attributes. Indeed, so taken for granted

179

is the belief in the importance of appearance that it functions as a major impetus behind our increasingly ready supplications to various experts in the body trades to correct whatever physical quirks we see as being social burdens. In short, so convinced are we of the importance of appearance that it gives credence to certain irrational behaviours – such as seeking a face lift to rejuvenate appearance, rigorous dieting to produce sexual attractiveness, spending disproportionate amounts of time and money on the purchase of fashionable items through which we hope to become enviable to and distinctive from others.

The self-evident truth that appearance matters has garnered to itself a great deal of supportive psychological test data. Facial deformities have frequently been found to have dramatic social consequences (Lefebvre and Munro 1986:53–62). In a review of psychological material which tested for connections between physical appearance and the stereotyping of personal characteristics, Dion (1986) found that close connections were repeatedly made, particularly with regard to women. Women were expected to be more attractive and to take greater care of their physical appearance than men. Support for such a view is easily found in the popular media, where major articles on women's beauty are commonplace. A recent cover story on the working older woman stated, 'forty isn't old any more. It's a fabulous time for women. You have press-on nails, you can change the colour of your eyes with contact lenses that you can throw away, you can have implants for cheeks, you can have your nose fixed, you can have your teeth bonded, you can change the colour of your hair. It's fantastic what a woman can do' (McCarthy 1989:62).

That appearance counts is not a new idea; only the specific edicts, to be blonde or thin or athletic or natural or young, are continuously new. For example, the current ideal in appearance in the industrialized West deems that women should be thinner and men should be taller. It is significant, in this era where feminist ideas have to some extent altered the distribution of social prestige between the sexes, that these specific requirements entail vastly different efforts on the part of women and men. For instance, height is generally regarded as a fixed attribute whereas weight is thought to be alterable, albeit with some effort. Being tall is a happy circumstance over which one has relatively little control, but being heavy is entirely of one's own making. These cultural ideals of appearance have the effect of making women far more responsible for their physical appearance than are men. A short man is regarded as unlucky but an overweight woman is blamed for her size and, as such, becomes a target of derision. DeJong and Kleck (1986:66) maintain that women who are overweight are further stigmatized by the attribution of other characteristics; 'the overweight not only do not have an acceptable physical appearance but are also perceived as characterologically flawed for not being able to resist the temptation of food.' Thus, being fat has become a statement of character, but more importantly, a revelation of one's weaknesses of character (1986:75). The halo effect, which explains why attractive people are gratuitously assigned other valued attributes, can be seen to work in reverse for the overweight who are instead attributed with deficits of character. So, if an overweight woman finds these attributes distressing, then her options are clear, she must alter her appearance. Alleviating the stigma of being overweight, or trying to avoid it altogether, has encouraged a growth in health industries and products such as diet farms, diet books, pills and plans, low calorie foods, home gymnasiums, exercise machines and other body-fashioning techniques. As well, medical interventions have developed, such as the intestinal bypass or stomach stapling (Solow 1977) and the various other cosmetic and plastic procedures outlined in chapter 3.

The specific cultural ideals of physical appearance are subject to the vagaries of fashion. Clark's (1980) history of Western aesthetics has clearly demonstrated that the ideal of the female shape has altered significantly. Until the seventeenth century, for example, the ideal female size was by modern standards plump and relatively large. Banner (1983) has pointed out that the 1921 winner of the first American beauty contest would be considered overweight by our contemporary standards. Garner *et al.* (1980) have reported that in the two decades from 1960 to 1980, the ideal appearance of women has become significantly thinner. Before 1970, women contestants in the Miss World beauty contest weighed 87.6 per cent of the average but, after

1970, this had declined to 84.6 per cent. In the twenty-year period of their study, the national average weight of women under thirty years of age had increased by five pounds, yet the ideal, promulgated through the media and fashion industries, had decreased. Garner *et al.* noted that the number of diet articles in the major women's popular magazines had increased in the 1970s by 10 per cent over the previous decade. Their conclusion was that the goal of the youth-worshipping American society had transposed the ideal woman's appearance into one that was more childlike in form, recalling once again the principle of neoteny discussed in chapter 2. It is an observation supported by Beller (1977) in her cross-cultural study of body shape. Whereas once a plump figure was a sign of health and wealth, particularly in subsistence societies, the current Western ideal is a light, swift body that expresses the strength of refusal and denial in an era where, ironically, luxury and superfluity abound.

Stewart and Brook (1983), in their study of the effects of being overweight, found that women more than men saw themselves as overweight, even when their weight was within normal actuarial limits. Similar observations that women are more concerned with their body shape have been made many times in recent literature (Millman 1980; Chernin 1981; Wooley 1982; Orbach 1986; Brumberg 1988). Without doubt, in our society, weight and body shape have a considerably stronger punitive effect on women than men (Dwyer 1973); indeed, men have much more flexibility with their size and shape. This is well illustrated by the clothing styles deemed appropriate for each sex. For instance, women's clothes are designed to emphasize the body, especially the hips and bosom, so, as a woman ages and her figure thickens, her extra weight is made more noticeable by her clothes (Garner *et al.* 1980). Conversely, as a man ages, he tends to add weight centrally where it can readily be concealed by the standard business suit.

That women are currently more vulnerable to culturally defined ideals of physical appearance is a reflection of their subordinate position. The status of men in industrialized societies is more closely attached to their labour value, and this

7 The Self as Sign

can account for their physical appearance being of secondary value. For women, however, their status has been historically tied to fluctuations in cultural definitions of beauty, femininity and sexual seductiveness (see Simmel 1984). In more recent times, as the cultural importance placed upon appearance has been further extended to include the male and, as men become more active consumers of fashion items, then it may well signify that the value and status of the male as worker have become precarious, and that men's claims to social superiority may be in jeopardy because of structural shifts in the economic order.

There are historical fluctuations in cultural ideals of physical attractiveness (Evans and Thornton 1989) but, although we tacitly understand that definitions of beauty and physical attractiveness are not enduring aesthetic concepts nor expressions of an idealism of the human form, it is still the case that we place a great deal of value on physical appearance in our reading of character. For Baudrillard, the answer to this paradox lies with the idiosyncratic demands made on the body by the prevailing norms of everyday sociality. He has persuasively argued that the social value of beauty in the contemporary era is unrelated to any ideals of physical attractiveness but is, instead, attached to the means by which the individual has been able to secure such an appearance of beauty or attractiveness (Baudrillard 1983). That is, the value of one's physical appearance rests upon its being interpreted as a measure of one's competence with the tools and devices which are available to transform and style the human body. Beauty is achieved and asserted; thus, one's physical appearance becomes an emblem of status and, in particular, one's ability to procure and possess what one wants. That is, the value of physical attractiveness and beauty relates more to the ways in which they were obtained; in contemporary society, it is the technology of appearance that is paramount, and being able to shape appearance in order to meet one's desires is what matters. This makes the value of 'tattoos, stretched lips, the bound feet of Chinese women, eyeshadow, rouge, hair removal, mascara, or bracelets, collars, objects, jewelry, accessories' rest upon the idea that they 'serve

183

to rewrite the cultural order on the body; and it is this that takes on the effect of beauty' (Baudrillard 1981:94).

The value of the individual's physical appearance lies not so much in its approximation to a specific style or ideal of beauty but as an indication of his or her willingness to treat the body as malleable, and to subject him- or herself to the array of tools and techniques that can fashion it. Thus, the social value of a particular style of appearance rests largely with its symbolizing one's willingness to reshape oneself at will, to regard oneself as a commodity.

Baudrillard's view is important because it indicates an element of the modern sensibility which highlights the thesis of this work, namely, that in our willingness to groom ourselves in any way that accords with prevailing fashions and customs, we are demonstrating the greater value we place upon appearances and upon the visible details of our persona, than upon more abstract qualities of human character which are cultivated over a life-time of rumination. When we emphasize physical appearance we are implicitly advocating a materialist eschatology applicable to the understanding of human character.

Wittgenstein (1967:178) maintained that the human body gave the best picture of the human soul and this, Baudrillard and Goffman would agree, is also true when that body has been disguised, say, with fashionable clothing or when it is masked with cosmetics. The 'human soul' that Wittgenstein has called the essence of human character is still the referent of the human body, especially so in the modern era when that body has been wilfully transformed. Wittgenstein's comments direct us to ask, when devices and techniques can be employed in the fashioning and refashioning of the body, does that mean that the 'human soul' or character is also considered to be manufactured with the same plastic quality? In other words, do we conceive of human character as if it were a commodity and capable, like other commodities, of being fashionable, *passé*, elegant or vulgar? The short answer, it seems, would be in the affirmative.

Baudrillard (1983) has depicted modern social life as dominated by the ephemera of images. Most often, these images are selected by the individual in much the same way that items of apparel or purchasable objects are selected, and then these images are employed as statements of one's character: 'I'm a member of the Pepsi generation'; 'I'm a Marlboro Man'. Such conduct is concordant with Goffman's analyses of sociality where individuals are continually engaged with the manufacture of images, roles and performances which, in turn, exude impressions which the individual wants to control. Goffman's work is a map of the various strategies followed by individuals in daily social exchanges. As such, Goffman has not produced a theory of self (Ditton 1980; Giddens 1987), but he has thoroughly described the manner in which the individual has produced an idea or image that is known as the self and which, subsequently, becomes an integral feature of the social encounter. It is in the enactment of the roles, scripts and regulated performances which we deem appropriate to the situation, that Goffman has shown where and how a sense of personal identity is produced. With physical appearance, for instance, he has described how the individual's sense of equilibrium and selfhood can be dramatically altered when his or her appearance is changed. In his analysis of the mortification process, where the individual's identity is destroyed by stripping off all items of clothing and personal effects, by shaving the head, imposing nudity and social isolation, Goffman has illustrated the importance of physical appearance to the assertion of personal identity (1961). Again, in his descriptions of the banalities of everyday social exchange, Goffman has made the same point that self-identity is interwoven with appearance and how others regard that appearance. What we want to demonstrate as a self is constructed from our physical attributes, our ability to enact the patterns of behaviour and roles that are culturally assigned to us and, most importantly, from our perceptions of how others see us, how they regard our physical appearance, manners, conversational style and so on. Identity is extracted from our ability to detect, in the minutiae of the social situation, the other's impressions of us and, in turn, to control those opinions (Goffman 1983).

Cooley (1902:87) had described the process more than half a century earlier; 'the imaginations which people have of one another are the solid facts of society'. That is, the signs of the self are taken as the self. Although Mead (1934:224) thought Cooley's position somewhat solipsistic because it gave no recognition to possible conflicts between the individual and society, nor to the possibility of spontaneous claims that could emanate from a dimension of the self he called the I, nonetheless, Cooley's concept of the mirror-glass self has a remarkably contemporary resonance. For instance, Goffman argued that social interaction is a product of the preparations that the individual has made in order to engage the other. The self is an image and its constituents are those devices used by the individual to present a self which can influence and control the reactions of the other.

For Goffman, the manner in which individuals engage one another, particularly face to face, gives emphasis to the relational element of human identity. For him, sociality is a process through which we secure an identity: the social act is a dialogue between what individuals intend to portray of themselves and what is unintentionally revealed (Goffman 1963). In the first moments of an interpersonal encounter, we seek to identify the other's gender, age and socio-economic status because we intentionally use these as programmatic cues to assist in the ensuing interaction. For instance, identifying gender immediately provides a repertoire or script for any exchange; this is also the case when we identify the other as old or young, rich or poor, black or white. From these obvious categorizations, we move to more abstract deductions. Again, in the early moments of engagement, we attempt to gauge the individual's own sense of self by working out whether s/he thinks of him- or herself as shy, confident, commanding, arrogant and so on. We want to know the others' self-image, how they see themselves, in order to anticipate the demands they may place upon us. Such knowledge may allow us to anticipate whether we will be carried along by their poise and mettle or whether we will be required to author the sociality ourselves, sometimes in the face of their maladroitness. In the initial moments of social engagement, we may ferret through bits of information and seize upon fleeting examples of the other's conduct that we interpret as accurate encapsulations of his or her broader identifying qualities. As we take a measure of the other's personal

186

qualities in this way, the social interaction subsequently becomes a struggle to control the impressions made and the
meanings derived from that exchange. As it is from these
elements of an individual's social conduct that a sense of identity is assembled, we come to think of the self as a concatenation
of signs. The self is thought of as an assemblage.

Goffman's dramaturgy gives a vivid account of how central
to sociality is the individual's ability to fashion and present
him- or herself to others. The structure of the exchange is all-
important. The concealed dimensions of rumination, where
doubt, anxiety, imagination, critique and boredom abide, are
not seen as all that important to the public conduct of social
life. Goffman's account of the labyrinthine efforts undertaken
by individuals in order to represent themselves as they wish to
be is a demonstration of the dependency that the individual has
on circumstance. It is as if the individual's sense of self were
synchronous with the demands of the situation, as if the individual and the social frame were complementary. As a result,
the modern individual gains a sense of him- or herself only as a
contingency. Goffman's world is a contestation of will and wit;
the face-to-face exchange is a mordant exercise in mutual manipulation and competition; there is no interest in a self other
than that which can be produced and presented to others.

The self as assemblage demonstrates time and time again how
little we value the contemplative and how much we value the
performative. This view shows that the modern self is contingent, that in the authenticating narrative of the contemporary
epoch, it has no enduring substance, it is simply treated as an
icon.

The view of the contingent self, which is attached to circumstances in a temporary, relativistic and fleeting relationship,
rests on a definition that the self is a fanfare of disguises and a
seemingly endless display of fashioned appearances. This view
of the self assumes a *homo clausus*. The consequences of this
perspective are exemplified in our willingness to commodify
sociality, emphasize self-interests and retreat from the exercise
of reflection and critique.

From a more transcendental perspective on identity, such as
that offered by Elias (1978), Steiner (1981) and Heller (1985),

our efforts to cultivate the self and acquire self-knowledge are activities which have had the unexpected effect of distancing us from the articulated object of our desires, namely, a developed sense of self. It is as if the more we have pursued a sense of identity, in the late twentieth century, the weaker that identity has become. Yet, to argue that there is no self or only an iconic self in an era where self-promotion is widely touted seems rather puzzling. Nonetheless, this is the point made by Morgenthau and Person (1978). They have argued through their exploration of modern narcissism, that the contingent self is an instrument in opposition to the development of subjectivity. The contemporary emphasis on self-promotion, self-presentation, self-regulation, self-realization, self-knowledge and so on has emerged from a misconceptualization of the individual's position in a society based on the rationalizing paradigm of the bureaucratic society. Morgenthau and Person (1978:337) have claimed that, while 'the celebration of the self has been a recurrent theme in western civilization ... viewed as compatible and even organically connected with a stable world order', the modern self diverges from this tradition and can no longer be regarded as a basis of social and personal stability. Instead, the idea of self has been made into an 'ultimate value', that is, it has been fashioned into a commodity, an entity of its own. While previous conceptualizations of identity and selfhood have subordinated it to social structures such as family, society and religion, now 'the ascendancy of the concern for self as an ultimate value is unmistakable', and it is this shift in emphasis which transforms the idea of self into a 'disintegrative element' (Morgenthau and Person 1978:337–9). The same perspective is broached by Baudrillard with his description of the self as an image and simulation which has been divorced from its referent; it is, furthermore, the conclusion offered by Goffman in his descriptions of the self as a momentary social product.

When an 'exalted notion of the self' (Morgenthau and Person 1978:344) comes to be generally held, and when the culture and therapeutic industries thrive by stressing the value of individual psychology, self-presentation, self-feeling, survivalism and hedonism, then an emphasis has been given to the singularity of the person. How one looks, feels, presents oneself and how well one understands one's proclivities and idiosyncracies, have been elevated in importance above one's abilities to act collectively or be engaged by the interests of a community. Thus, the value attributed to the representation of the self has the subversive effect of weakening the individual's interest in the political and communal activities of the public domain. When the character of an epoch or a particular society is not examined, when the individual becomes too self-absorbed, the danger is that political quietism will follow. Arendt (1968:4) has argued that when psychological effects are elevated in importance, and when the stature of individuals is measured by unique qualities thought to be internal to them, which are, also, seen as the origins of identity, then any understanding of the social and political has been occluded. Thus, in an era dominated by an emphasis on the representation of self and the public enunciation of singular concerns, the exercise of a realm of human subjectivity has become largely unknown. Sennett (1976:4) has commented that this desire 'to know oneself has become an end, instead of a means through which one knows the world.' Thus, it can be seen that the contemporary emphasis given to the self has the consequence of eroding the Enlightenment ideal of an egalitarian, democratic and humane society.

The subversion of the individual's self-knowledge or self-consciousness has come with the modern reification of the self. This ironic circumstance has not come about against our will. We have been induced into the world of images by the consumer ethic which has emphasized the physical body and the material object. The power we have learned to enjoy over ourselves, that allows us to shape our appearances through interventions such as surgery, cosmetics and body-shaping exercises, and the power we have gained to fashion our sensibilities and psychology through transforming experiences such as psychotherapy, make us think we also have the power to extend these transforming practices into the public realm of social circumstances. After all, if we can transform ourselves, we can surely use the same abilities to transform our place in the world. However, this turns out to be spurious logic; when the individual becomes the ultimate focus of attention and nurturance, and when a heightened or developed consciousness is sought through the cultivation of the body, then an era dawns in which only a partial understanding of collective social life can exist. In such a society, the continuity between the body politic and the private body has not been understood thoroughly enough to engender a sense of interest in those communal actions which are necessary for the progressive liberalization of a society.

As we saw in the previous chapter with George Konrad's modern individual, the discovery of the self through an immersion in an institutional framework is no longer possible because those sources of identity have become internally chaotic, disorganized and hostile to the individual. The emergence of an ethic of self-concern is not surprising, given that the capitalist society has made interpersonal competitiveness the norm. The contemporary individual is continually identifying him- or herself as a success or failure via momentary measures supplied by the competitive struggle for the control of goods and services (see Berman 1970). How can a sense of personal identity be forged in a social epoch where a sense of abiding character, one that is largely unresponsive to fashions and contingencies, receives little public attention or value?

If self-identity is produced and fashioned from commodities and images, if it is contingent on circumstances, then it has neither debt nor allegiance to communally shared values, historical concerns or transcendental aspirations. The emphasis given to the presentation of the self in our daily social life, and the proliferation of goods, services and techniques aimed at allowing us to produce a distinctive identity, have the effect of deflecting attention away from a more valuable source of identity, namely, the historical precedents and the immediate politics of our circumstances. Our current pursuit of the fashioned self commits us to a series of activities and interests which lodge us more firmly in a world remote from the on-going exigencies of political life. Our pursuit of the desired self-image takes place in a realm of the hyperreal where 'the industry of the Absolute Fake' produces 'a place of absolute iconism' (Eco 1986:48, 56). The ascendancy of the image has the capacity to deflect us from an interest in understanding that a society needs to be produced. The image as a mirror, representation of and counterpart to the real, also acts to contaminate reality; thus, the approximation of the image to reality can distort and even supersede that reality (see Baudrillard 1986; 1987).

The constant demand to live out the appropriate images and role demands of the everyday does not provide any real sustenance for the self. Instead, it leads to a self fabricated from an image which will collapse or implode under the weight of the never-satisfied desires which are pressed upon individuals from the consumer culture. It is much the same idea that Sennett expressed in his descriptions of the modern industrial society where the idea of the self took on such inflated proportions that it became susceptible to atrophy. Our current pathological condition of political and historical myopia is a result of our passion for identity and our inflated evaluation of the self. The consequence is a form of narcissism which is so enthralling that it effectively blocks out or, at minimum, dilutes the influences of others. In effect, the pursuit of the self does not produce a self, it only produces an image or simulation of a self which finally has the effect of subverting its own referent and the social impetus.

Baudrillard and Eco independently argue that the broadly held commonsensical understandings of personal identity are misconceived because they make the concept of self seem an entity lodged within the individual as if it were an independent phenomenon; the image is of the *homo clausus*. Thus, the icons constantly displayed before us in the mass media of happy, successful, active people who have a sense of their own destiny, are frequently misread as realistic depictions of human character. We are cajoled to emulate the sporting hero, the owner of the American Express credit card, the energetic members of the Pepsi generation, but these images are insubstantial. The pursuit of the identity represented as desirable by these images is both hectoring and misleading, and were the individual to adopt these postures fully, s/he would become socially naive and inept.

The image of the self promulgated in the post-industrial, consumer culture is automatically remote from its referent.

191

The historical and cultural ideal of the self, which transcends appearances, has been overshadowed by the images of the contemporary self which stridently emphasizes the opposite, namely, the importance of appearances. The image continues to attain new heights of importance, and its proliferation has the effect of imposing a ready-made meaning over social events and acts which are, by nature, more fluid and contestatory. To claim a sense of identity from a social horizon of fashioned images, is to make the self merely a repository and concatenation of discrete elements. The interior has been furnished from the exterior. As such, the individual's sense of possessing a unique sense of identity is only another constituent element in the authenticating narrative of the times. The idea of the self being sought is not original, but is drawn from the plethora of images found in the publicized enactments of everyday life. It is a self which resembles every other self, it is a self in imitation of the other. The new hegemony of appearance, where the presentation of self is taken as the self, signals a failure to understand the relationship between the individual and the other. The development of an authentic self now rests with our discovery that the self we commonly aspire to is an image also aspired to by everyone else.

In the modern age, the value of appearance has been grossly inflated; by attaching human character to physical appearance we now use the constructed, styled, fashioned image as a summary of personal identity. It is as if personal identity has been re-conceptualized as a sign or image. In such circumstances, the reading of human character can be abbreviated to a cursory review of the individual's appearance and possessions. This viewpoint determines that personal identity is visible and self-evident, and the consequence is that we have little need to reflect on or consider what is identity. When we accept the visible and treat it as if it were self-revealing, then we have entered the realm of the despotic banal. Questions that may be suggested about the nature of personal identity are left neglected and under-explored. There is no public discourse on the relationship of the self to society; thus, when we claim to know someone's character, it is probably a matter of intuition or clever assumption rather than a knowledge derived from the exercise of well-used tools of critique.

Our preoccupation with self-feeling and self-knowledge, rather than indicating a renewed interest in rumination as the source from which an authentic experience of subjectivity can emerge, suggests, instead, the ascendancy of the imagined and fashioned self which prizes performance over all else. This is the understanding of selfhood which Daisy de Bellefeuille expressed with her desire for the transformative face lift.

The face lift, the reshaping of the external, the image of beauty regained, had for Daisy the power to transpose her worries and anxieties about her place in the world into a tangible solution. Her doubts over the meaning of her life could be answered, even if temporarily, with an alteration in appearance. It could not be argued that Daisy's capacity for thought had evaporated, rather, it can be concluded that, in the era of the fashioned self, the opportunities provided by the culture and therapeutic industries for a transforming experience have successfully drawn the individual to the surface of life, away from the labyrinths of the subjective and ruminative.

From a study of the modern, fashioned self and those elements of the material culture which are employed to style a self-image, we are alerted to the prevailing views of what is meant by human character or identity. It would seem, in the modern consumer-oriented society, that we can satisfy ourselves with a sense of knowing the other by observing their appearance and manners of public conduct. We employ, unwittingly, a reworked physiognomy that allows us to see the other in their physical features. At the same time, we have become accustomed to the tyrannies of fashion but have not rejected the ever-renewed sameness of the objects and ideas that homogenize us. The sign, the fashion, the new, the well-presented, have become so distracting, so successfully deflecting of curiosity and the capacity for critique, that we accept the surface as if it were all there was. As in Oscar Wilde's parable of Dorian Gray, the picture has become the reality, the world has been reduced to the visible, the self has been confused with its image.

Bibliography

Adams, J. C. 1961. *The Globe Playhouse: Its Design and Equipment.* Constable, London.

Alford, C. F. 1988. *Narcissism.* Yale University Press, New Haven.

Alley, T. R. 1980. Infantile colouration as an elicitor of caretaking behaviour in old world primates. *Primates.* 21, 416–29.

Alvarez, A. 1989. This man is no tailor's dummy. *The Sunday Times Magazine.* 16 April, 19–22.

American Foundation for Craniofacial Deformities. n.d., Dallas, Texas.

Arbus, D. 1972. *Diane Arbus.* Aperture Monograph, New York.

Arendt, H. 1947. *Rahel Varnhagen: The Life of a Jewish Woman* Harcourt, New York.

Arendt, H. 1968. *Men In Dark Times.* Harcourt, New York.

Ariès, P. 1962. *Centuries of Childhood.* Vintage Books, New York.

'Aristotelis philosophi phisnomia.' 14th cent. British Library, Sloane MS 3469.

Aristotle. 1943. *Generation of Animals.* Translated A. Peck. Harvard University Press, Cambridge, Mass.

Baker, T. J. and H. L. Gordon 1980. Effects of the chemical peel. In Goldwyn 1980. 628–40.

Banner, L. 1983. *American Beauty.* University of Chicago Press, Chicago.

Barber, B. and L. Lobel 1953. Fashion in women's clothes and the American social system. In R. Bendix and S. Lipset (eds) *Class, Status and Power.* Free Press, New York. 323–32.

Bibliography

Barbu, Z. 1960. *Problems of Historical Psychology*. Routledge and Kegan Paul, London.

Barnes, D. 1936. *Nightwood*. Faber and Faber, London.

Barrow, M. V. 1971. A brief history of teratology to the early C20th *Teratology*. 4, 119–30.

Barthes, R. 1973. *Mythologies*. Paladin, London.

Barthes, R. 1985. *The Fashion System*. Jonathan Cape, London.

Baudrillard, J. 1979. *De la séduction*. Galilée, Paris.

Baudrillard, J. 1981. *For a Critique of the Political Economy of the Sign*. Telos, St Louis, Missouri.

Baudrillard, J. 1983. *Simulations*. Semiotext(e), New York.

Baudrillard, J. 1985. The ecstasy of communication. In H. Foster (ed.) *Postmodern Culture*. Pluto Press, London. 126–34.

Baudrillard, J. 1986. The year 2000 will not take place. In E. A. Grosz, T. Threadgold, D. Kelly, A. Cholodenko and E. Colless (eds) *Futur*Fall: Excursions into Post-Modernity*. Power Institute Publications, Sydney. 18–28.

Baudrillard, J. 1987. *The Evil Demon of Images*. Power Institute Publications, Sydney.

Baudrillard, J. 1988. *Selected Writings*. Edited and introduced by M. Poster. Stanford University Press, Stanford.

Bell, Q. 1976. *On Human Finery*. Hogarth Press, London.

Beller, A. 1977. *Fat and Thin*. Farrar, Straus and Giroux, New York.

Bellière, de la C. 'Physionomia Rationalis.' Translated into English by Robert Baker. 17th cent. British Library, Sloane MS 3942.

Berlin, I. 1969. A note on Vico's concept of knowledge. In G. Tagliacozzo and H. White (eds) *Giambattista Vico: An International Symposium*. Johns Hopkins Press, Baltimore. 374–80.

Berman, M. 1970. *The Politics of Authenticity*. Atheneum, New York.

Berry, E. P. 1980. Levels of satisfaction in the face lift and eyelid operations. In Goldwyn 1980. 664–73.

Betterton, R. (ed.) 1987. *Looking On*. Pandora Press, London.

Blackburne, Professor. 1881. *Love, Courtship and Marriage (Phrenologically Considered) With Useful Hints How To Make a Wise Choice, and Thus Live Happily through Life*. Harrison and Waide, Bridge End, Leeds.

Blumer, H. 1968. Fashion. In D. Sills (ed.) *International Encyclopedia of the Social Sciences*. Macmillan and Free Press, New York. 341–45.

Blumer, H. 1969. Fashion: from class differentiation to collective selection. *Sociological Quarterly*. 10, 275–91.

Bibliography

Bolk, L. 1929. Origin of racial characteristics in man. *American Journal of Physical Anthropology*. 13, 1–28.

Boo-Chai, K. 1963. Plastic construction of the superior palpebral fold. *Plastic and Reconstructive Surgery*. 31, 74.

Boo-Chai, K. 1964. Augmentation rhinoplasty in the Oriental. *Plastic and Reconstructive Surgery*. 34, 81.

Bostwick III, J. 1981. Breast reconstruction following radical mastectomy. In I. T. Jackson (ed.) *Recent Advances in Plastic Surgery 2*. Churchill Livingstone, Edinburgh. 1–9.

Boucher, F. 1967. *A History of Costume*. Thames and Hudson, London.

Bourdieu, P. 1984. *Distinction. A Social Critique of the Judgement of Taste*. Harvard University Press, Cambridge, Mass.

Bowlby, R. 1985. *Just Looking*. Methuen, London and New York.

Boyne, R. 1988. The art of the body in the discourse of postmodernity. *Theory, Culture and Society*. 5(2–3): 527–42.

Braudel, F. 1981. *The Structures of Everyday Life*. vol. 1. Harper and Row, New York.

Braudel, F. 1982. *The Wheels of Commerce*. vol. 2. Harper and Row, New York.

Braunstein, P. 1988. Toward intimacy: The fourteenth and fifteenth centuries. In G. Duby 1988a. 535–630.

Brenninkmeyer, I. 1962. *The Sociology of Fashion*. P. G. Keller, Winterthur.

Bretteville-Jensen, G., N. Mossing and R. Albrechtsen 1975. Surgical treatment of axillary hyperhidrosis in 123 patients. *Acta Dermato-venereologica*. 55, 73–7.

Broadbent, T. R. and R. M. Woolf 1980. Cosmetic rhinoplasty. In Goldwyn 1980. 532–47.

Broca, P. 1866. Anthropologie. In A. Dechambre (ed.) *Dictionnaire encyclopédique des sciences médicales*. Masson, Paris. 276–300.

Broca, P. 1876. *Le programme de l'anthropologie*. Cusset, Paris.

Brodsky, I. 1943. Congenital abnormalities, teratology and embryology: some evidence of primitive man's knowledge as expressed in art and lore in Oceania. *Medical Journal of Australia*. 1, 417.

Bruch, H. 1978. *The Golden Cage*. Open Books, Somerset.

Brumberg, J. J. 1988. *Fasting Girls: The Emergence of Anorexia Nervosa as a Modern Disease*. Harvard University Press, Cambridge, Mass.

Bunker, J. P. 1985. When doctors disagree. *New York Review of Books*. 25 April.

Bibliography

Bürger, P. 1986. *Theory of the Avant-Garde*. University of Minnesota Press, Wisconsin.

Byatt, A. S. 1986. *Still Life*. Penguin, Middlesex.

Cahnman, W. J. 1968. The stigma of obesity. *Sociological Quarterly*. 9, 283–99.

Cardano, G. 1658. *Metoposcopia*: 16th cent. British Library 719 m. 11 (abbreviated German translation 1695. British Library 8630. bbb. 11.).

Carlyle, T. 1834. *Sartor Resartus*. Ward, Locke and Co., London.

Castanares, S. 1980. The brow lift. In Goldwyn 1980. 644–51.

Chambers Biographical Dictionary. 1969. St. Martin's, New York.

Chaney, D. 1983. The department store as a cultural form. *Theory, Culture and Society*. 1(3): 22–31.

Chernin, K. 1981 *The Obsession: Reflections on the Tyranny of Slenderness*. Harper and Row, New York.

Chorover, S. 1979. *From Genesis to Genocide*, MIT Press, Cambridge, Mass.

Clark, K. 1980. *Feminine Beauty*. Rizzoli, New York.

Colen, B. D. 1976. *Karen Ann Quinlan: Dying in an Age of Eternal Life*. Nash Books, New York.

Connell, B. F. 1985. Finesse in rhytidectomy. In I. T. Jackson and B. C. Sommerlad (eds) *Recent Advances in Plastic Surgery No. 3*. Churchill Livingstone, Edinburgh, 137–56.

Cooley, C. H. 1902. *Human Nature and the Social Order*. Scribner, New York.

Cordwell, J. and R. Schwarz (eds) 1979. *The Fabrics of Culture: The Anthropology of Clothing and Adornment*. The Hague, Mouton.

Cosmetics and Toiletries Report. 1985. 3rd edition. Researched and published by Euromonitor Publications, London.

Craig, H. 1915. *The Works of John Metham*. Kegan Paul, Trench, Trübner and Co., London.

Cruse, E. 1874. *Phrenology Made Easy, or the Art of Studying Character*. W. H. Elliot, London.

Dallmayr, F. 1981. *Twilight of Subjectivity*. University of Massachusetts Press, Amherst.

Darwin, C. 1872 (1965). *The Expression of the Emotions in Man and Animals*. University of Chicago Press, Chicago.

Davis, F. 1961. Deviance disavowal. *Social Problems*. 11, 12–32.

Davis, F. 1985. Clothing and fashion as communication. In M. Solomon (ed.) *The Psychology of Fashion*. Lexington Books, D. C. Heath, Massachusetts and Toronto. 15–27.

197

Bibliography

Debord, G. 1977. *The Society of the Spectacle*. Red and Black, Detroit.

DeJong, W. and R. E. Kleck 1986. The social psychological effects of overweight. In Herman *et al.* 1986. 65–87.

de la Mare, W. 1921 (1955). *Memoirs of a Midget*. Penguin, Middlesex.

de Marly, D. 1985. *Fashion for Men*. B. T. Batsford, London.

Denzin, N. 1984. *On Understanding Emotion*. Jossey-Bass, San Francisco.

Dickens, C. 1841 (1972). *The Old Curiosity Shop*. Penguin, Middlesex.

Dion, K. 1986. Stereotyping based on physical attractiveness: issues and conceptual perspectives. In Herman *et al.* 1986. 7–21.

Ditton, J. 1980. *The View From Goffman*. Macmillan, London.

Douglas, M. 1973. *Natural Symbols*. Penguin, Middlesex.

Duby, G. (ed.) 1988a. *A History of Private Life*. vol 2. Belknap Press, Harvard University Press, Cambridge and London.

Duby, G. 1988b. Solitude: The eleventh to thirteenth centuries. In Duby 1988a 509–34.

Duff, R. S. and A. G. M. Campbell 1973. Moral and ethical dilemmas in the special care nursery. *New England Journal of Medicine*. 289. 890–4.

Duff, R. S. and A. G. M. Campbell 1979. Social perspectives on medical decisions relating to life and death. In J. Ladd (ed.) *Ethical Issues Relating to Life and Death*. Oxford University Press, Oxford.

Dumont, L. 1986. *Essays on Individualism*. University of Chicago Press, Chicago.

Dworkin, A. 1974. *Woman Hating*. E. P. Dutton, New York.

Dwyer, J. T. 1973. Psychosexual aspects of weight control and dieting behavior in adolescents. In Lief 1975. 82–108.

Eckstein, E. and G. Firkins 1987. *Gentlemen's Dress Accessories*. Album 205, Shire Publications, Aylesbury, Buckinghamshire.

Eco, U. 1979. *A Theory of Semiotics*. Indiana University Press, Bloomington.

Eco, U. 1986. *Faith In Fakes*. Secker and Warburg, London.

Eiseman, G. 1975. Surgical treatment of axillary hyperhidrosis as outpatient procedure. *Cutis*. 16, 69–72.

Elias, N. 1978. *The Civilizing Process*. Urizen, New York.

Elias, N. 1982. *Power and Civility*. Blackwell, Oxford.

Ellenbogen, R., R. Ellenbogen and L. Rubin 1975. Injectable fluid silicone therapy: human morbidity and mortality. *Journal of American Medical Association.* 234, 308–9.

Ellis, H. 1894. *Man and Woman.* Scribner, New York.

Ellmann, R. 1988. *Oscar Wilde.* Knopf, New York.

Elster, J. (ed.) 1986. *The Multiple Self.* Cambridge University Press, Cambridge.

Evans, C. and M. Thornton 1989. *Women and Fashion: A New Look.* Quartet Books, London and New York.

Fahoun, K. 1987. Skin lifting techniques in rhytidectomy. *Acta Chirurgiae Plasticae.* 29(2): 88–92.

Fahoun, K. 1988. Blepharoplasty of the lower eyelids, *Acta Chirurgiae Plasticae.* 30(1): 10–13.

Fallon, A. and R. Rozin 1985. Sex difference in the perception of desirable body shape. *Journal of Abnormal Psychology.* 94, 102–5.

Featherstone, M. 1987. Lifestyle and consumer culture. *Theory, Culture and Society.* 4(1): 55–70.

Fernald, W. E. 1976. The imbecile with criminal instincts. In M. Rosen, G. R. Clark and M. S. Kivitz (eds) *The History of Mental Retardation. Collected Papers 2.* Baltimore University Park Press, Baltimore. 167–83.

Fiedler, L. 1981. *Freaks: Myths and Images of the Secret Self.* Penguin, Middlesex.

Finkelstein, J. 1989. *Dining Out: A Sociology of Modern Manners.* Polity, Cambridge.

Fletcher, J. 1974. Attitudes toward defective newborns. *Hastings Center Studies.* 2, 21–32.

Fletcher, J. 1975. Moral and ethical problems of prenatal diagnosis. *Clinical Genetics.* 8, 251–7.

Flügel, J. C. 1930. *The Psychology of Clothes.* Hogarth Press, London.

Foerster, R. 1893. *Scriptores Physiognomici Graeci et Latini.* 2 vol. B. G. Teubner, Leipzig.

Foucault, M. 1970. *The Order of Things.* Tavistock, London.

Foucault, M. 1973. *Birth of the Clinic.* Tavistock, London.

Foucault, M. 1977. *Discipline and Punish: The Birth of the Prison.* Pantheon, New York.

Foucault, M. 1980. *Power/Knowledge.* Harvester Press, Sussex.

Foucault, M. 1983. *This Is Not A Pipe.* University of California Press, Berkeley.

Foucault, M. 1988. *Technologies of the Self.* Tavistock, London.

Bibliography

Fox, R. W. and T. J. Lears (eds) 1983. *The Culture of Consumption.* Pantheon, New York.

Frank, H. and Frank, M. G. 1982. On the effects of domestication on canine social behavior. *Applied Animal Ethology.* 8, 507–22.

Fraser, K. 1981. *The Fashionable Mind.* Knopf, New York.

Fraser, K. 1987. *Scenes From The Fashionable World.* Knopf, New York.

Fredricks, S. 1974. Lower rhytidectomy. *Plastic and Reconstructive Surgery.* 54, 537–43.

Freud, S. 1927. Fetishism. In J. Strachey (ed.) *The Standard Edition of the Complete Psychological Works of Sigmund Freud.* Hogarth Press, London. 1964. Vol. 21, 147–58.

Frontline 1983. No. 110. *Daisy: The story of a facelift.* PBS TV, 28 March.

Fussell, P. 1984. *Caste Marks.* Heinemann, London.

Garfinkel, H. 1956. Conditions of successful degradation ceremonies. *American Journal of Sociology.* 61, 420–4.

Garner, D. M., P. E. Garfinkel, D. Schwartz and M. Thompson 1980. Cultural expectations of thinness in women. *Psychological Reports.* 47, 483–91.

Giannini, M. J. and L. Goodman 1963. Counselling families during the crisis reaction to mongolism. *American Journal of Mental Deficiency.* 67, 743–4.

Giddens, A. 1987. *Social Theory and Modern Sociology.* Polity, Cambridge.

Gillies, Sir H. and D. R. Millard, Jnr. 1957. *The Principles and Art of Plastic Surgery.* vols. 1 and 2. Butterworth, London.

Girouard, M. 1980. *Life In The English Country House.* Penguin, Middlesex.

Gissing, G. 1977 (1893). *The Odd Women.* W. W. Norton, New York.

Glover, J. 1977. *Causing Death and Saving Lives.* Penguin, Middlesex.

Goffman, E. 1959. *The Presentation of Self in Everyday Life.* Penguin, Middlesex.

Goffman, E. 1961. *Asylums.* Anchor, New York.

Goffman, E. 1963. *Stigma. Notes on the Management of Spoiled Identity.* Penguin, Middlesex.

Goffman, E. 1967. *Interaction Ritual.* Anchor, New York.

Goffman, E. 1983. The interaction order. *American Sociological Review.* 48, 1–17.

Goldsmith, A. 1990. *Gracious Living.* Penguin, Ringwood.

Bibliography

Goldwyn, R. M. (ed.) 1980. *Long-Term Results in Plastic and Reconstructive Surgery*. Little, Brown & Co., Boston.

Gombrich, E. H. 1968. Style. In D. Sills (ed.) *International Encyclopedia of the Social Sciences*. Macmillan and Free Press, New York. 352–61.

Gould, G. M. and W. L. Pyke 1896. *Anomalies and Curiosities of Medicine*. Bell Publishing, New York.

Gould, S. J. 1980. *Ever Since Darwin*. Pelican, Middlesex.

Gould, S. J. 1983. *The Panda's Thumb*. Pelican, Middlesex.

Gould, S. J. 1984. *The Mismeasure of Man*. Pelican, Middlesex.

Grazer, F., J. Klingbeil and M. Mattiello 1980. Abdominoplasty. In Goldwyn 1980. 748–72.

Harris, F. (forthcoming). *A Passion for Government: the life of Sarah, Duchess of Marlborough*. Oxford University Press, Oxford.

Hart, A. D. n.d. *English Men's Fashionable Dress 1600–1799*. Department of Textiles and Dress, Victoria and Albert Museum, London.

Harvey, W. 1651. *Exercises on the Generation of Animals*. Jansson, Amsterdam.

Haug, W. F. 1986. *Critique of Commodity Aesthetics*. Polity, Cambridge.

Hazlitt, W. C. (ed.) 1892. *M. E. Montaigne (1580–8). Essays*. A. L. Burt & Co, New York.

Heilbrun, C. 1989. *Writing a Woman's Life*. Women's Press, London.

Heller, A. 1985. *The Power of Shame*. Routledge and Kegan Paul, London.

Heller, A. 1989. Contingent Person and Existential Choice. *The Philosophical Forum*. 21(1–2): 53–69.

Herman, C. P., M. Zanna, E. T. Higgins (eds) 1986. *Physical Appearance, Stigma, and Social Behavior*. Lawrence Erlbaum Associates, New Jersey and London.

Hirshowitz, B. 1978. The two-stage face lift. *British Journal of Plastic Surgery*. 31, 159.

Hochschild, A. 1983. *The Managed Heart*. University of California Press, Berkeley.

Hollander, A. 1980. *Seeing Through Clothes*. Avon, New York.

Homer 1974. *The Odyssey*. Translated by A. Cook. W. W. Norton, New York.

Horne, M. J. 1967. *The Second Skin: An Interdisciplinary Study of Clothing*. Houghton Mifflin, Boston.

Bibliography

Hugo, V. 1831 (1956). *The Hunchback of Notre Dame*. Bantam, New York.

Hugo, V. 1862 (1964). *Les Misérables*. Washington Square Press, New York.

Hugo, V. 1887. *The Laughing Man*. Routledge, London.

Huizinga, J. 1952. *Homo Ludens*. Paladin, London.

Illich, I. 1975. *Medical Nemesis*. Calder and Boyars, London.

Indagine, J. ab. 1666. *The Book of Palmestry and Physiognomy*. Translated into English by Fabian Withers. 6th ed. Thomas Passenger, London Bridge.

Jacobson, W. E., M. T. Edgerton, E. Meyer, A. Canter and R. Slaughter 1960. Psychiatric evaluation of male patients seeking cosmetic surgery. *Plastic and Reconstructive Surgery*. 26, 356–72.

Jacoby, R. 1975. *Social Amnesia*. Beacon Press, Boston.

Jacoby, R. 1971. The politics of subjectivity. *Telos*. 9, 20–7.

Jewson, N. D. 1976. The disappearance of the sick man from medical cosmology 1770–1870. *Sociology*. 10, 225–44.

Kahn, S. and B. Simon 1980. Meloplasty. In Goldwyn 1980. 678–92.

Kaye, B. L. 1980. The forehead lift. In Goldwyn 1980. 654– 62.

Keating, J. M. 1889. *Cyclopaedia of Diseases of Children*. J. B. Lippincott, Philadelphia.

Kennedy, I. 1981. *The Unmasking of Medicine*. Allen and Unwin, London.

Kennell, J. H. and M. H. Klaus 1971. Care of the mother of the high risk infant. *Clinical Obstetrics and Gynecology*. 14, 928–40.

Knorr, N. J., J. E. Hoopes and M. T. Edgerton 1968. Psychiatric-surgical approach to adolescent disturbance of self-image. *Plastic and Reconstructive Surgery*. 41, 248–53.

Konrad, G. 1975. *The Case Worker*. Hutchinson and Co., London.

Kryslova, I. and K. Fahoun 1988. Corrective otoplasty. *Acta Chirurgiae Plasticae*. 30(2): 105–12.

Kunzle, D. 1982. *Fashion and Fetishism: A Social History of the Corset, Tight-Lacing and other Forms of Body Sculpture in the West*. Rowan and Totowa, New Jersey.

Lakoff, R. T. and R. L. Scherr 1984. *Face Value: The Politics of Beauty*. Routledge, Kegan and Paul, Boston and London.

Lasch, C. 1979. *The Culture of Narcissism*. W. W. Norton, New York.

Laslett, P. 1965. *The World We Have Lost: England Before the Industrial Age*. Scribner, New York.

Lavater, J. C. 1775–8 (1804). *Essays on Physiognomy*. 4 vols.

Bibliography

Translated T. Holcroft from *Physiognomische Fragmente zur Beförderung der Menschenkenntniss und Menschenliebe*. Leipsig and Winterthur.

Lavater, J. C. 1793. 'Mélanges des regles Physiognomiques.' British Library, Additional MS 16403–16404.

Lavater, J. C. 1885. *Essays on Physiognomy*. Translated T. Holcroft. 19th edition. Ward, Lock and Bowden Ltd., London.

Laver, J. 1969. *A Concise History of Costume*. Thames and Hudson, London.

Lefebvre, A. and I. R. Munro 1986. Psychological adjustment of patients with craniofacial deformities before and after surgery. In Herman *et al*. 1986. 53–62.

Levi, P. 1987. *If This Be A Man*. Abacus, London.

Levi, P. 1989. *The Drowned and the Saved*. Vintage, New York.

Lewis, J. R. Jr. 1980. Surgery of the hips, buttocks and thighs. In Goldwyn 1980. 774–89.

Lewontin, R. C., S. Rose and L. J. Kamin 1984. *Not In Our Genes: Biology, Ideology and Human Nature*. Pantheon, New York.

Lief, H. (ed.) 1975. *Medical Aspects of Human Sexuality*. Wilkin and Wilkin, Baltimore.

Linden, E. 1979. *Affluence and Discontent*. Viking, New York.

Lombroso, C. 1876. *L'uomo Delinquente*. Translated 1887 as *L'homme criminel*. F. Alcan, Paris.

Lombroso, C. 1911. *Crime: Its Causes and Remedies*. Little, Brown, Boston.

Lorber, J. 1974. Selective treatment of myelomeningocele: to treat or not to treat. *Pediatrics*. 53(3): 307–8.

Lorenz, K. 1950. *Studies in Animal and Human Behavior*. Vol. 2. Harvard University Press, Cambridge, Mass.

Lurie, A. 1983. *The Language of Clothes*. Vintage Books, New York.

Lynes, R. 1949. *The Tastemakers*. Harper and Row, New York.

Lyotard, J-F. 1987. *The Postmodern Condition: A Report On Knowledge*. Manchester, University Press, Manchester.

MacGregor, F. C. 1967. Social and cultural components in the motivations of persons seeking plastic surgery of the nose. *Journal of Health and Social Behaviour*. 8, 125–35.

MacGregor, F. C. 1973. Social and psychological considerations. In T. Rees and D. Wood-Smith (eds) 1973. 27–33.

MacIntyre, A. 1975. How virtues become vices: values, medicine and social context. In H. T. Englehardt and S. F. Spicker (eds) *Evaluation and Explanation in the Biomedical Sciences*. D. Reidel, Dodrecht. 97–111.

Bibliography

Magli, P. 1989. The face and the soul. In M. Feher, R. Naddaff and N. Tazi (eds) *Fragments for a History of the Human Body*. Part 2. Zone, MIT Press, Cambridge, Mass. 87–127.

Mahfouz, N. 1947 (1975). *Midaq Alley*. Heinemann, London.

Mantegazza, P. n.d. *Physiognomy and Expression*. Contemporary Science Series edited by Havelock Ellis. Walter Scott, London.

Marcuse, H. 1964. *One Dimensional Man*. Routledge and Kegan Paul, London.

Marwick, A. 1988. *Beauty in History: Society, Politics and Personal Appearance c.1500 to the Present*. Thames and Hudson, London.

McCarthy, P. 1989. Working rich New York style. *The Age Good Weekend*, Melbourne, 19 August, 56–62.

McCoy, F. J. (ed.) 1977. *Year Book of Plastic and Reconstructive Surgery*. Year Book Medical Publishing, Chicago.

McCracken, G. 1985. The trickle-down theory rehabilitated. In M. Solomon 1985. 39–54.

McKendrick, N., J. Brewer, J. H. Plumb 1982. *The Birth of a Consumer Society*. Europa, London.

Mead, G. H. 1934. *Mind Self and Society*. University of Chicago Press, Chicago.

Meredith, B. 1988. *A Change for the Better*. Grafton Books, London.

Millard Jr., D. R. 1974. Aesthetic rhinoplasty. In M. Saad and P. Lichtveld (eds) *Reviews in Plastic Surgery: General Plastic and Reconstructive Surgery*. American Elsevier, New York. 371–86.

Miller, M. 1981. *The Bon Marché: Bourgeois Culture and the Department Store 1869–1920*. Princeton University Press, New Jersey.

Millman, M. 1980. *Such a Pretty Face*. W. W. Norton & Co., New York.

Minchinton, W. 1982. Convention, fashion and consumption. In H. Baudet and H. van der Meulen (eds) *Consumer Behaviour and Economic Growth in the Modern Economy*. Croom Helm, London. 209–30.

Moers, E. 1978. *The Dandy*. University of Nebraska Press, Lincoln.

Molloy, J. 1975. *Dress for Success*. Warner Books, New York.

Molloy, J. 1977. *The Woman's Dress for Success Book*. Follett, Chicago.

Mondeville, de H. 1897–8. *La Chirurgie de Maitre Henri de Mondeville*. Edited by A. Bos. Librairie de Firmin Didot, Paris.

Montagu, A. 1974. *The Natural Superiority of Women*. Macmillan, New York.

Morgenthau, H. and E. Person 1978. The roots of narcissism. *Partisan Review*. 3, 337–47.

Bibliography

Mourad, Y. 1939. *La Physiognomie arabe et le Kitab al-Firasa de Fakhr al-Din al-Razi.* P. Geuthner, Paris.

Nabokov, V. 1958. *Nabakov's Dozen: Thirteen Stories.* Penguin, Middlesex.

Nellans, R. E., W. Naftel, J. Stein, L. Tansey, J. Perley and J. Ravera 1976. Experience with the small-carrion penile prosthesis in treatment of organic impotence. *Journal of Urology.* 115, 280–3.

Orbach, S. 1986. *Hunger Strike.* Faber and Faber, London.

Ortner, S. and H. Whitehead (eds) 1981. *Sexual Meanings.* Cambridge University Press, Cambridge.

Pack, R. A. 1974. Auctoris incerti *De physiognomonia* libellus. *Archives D'Histoire Doctrinale et Littéraire du Moyen Age.* British Library, pamphlet 2278. 113–38

Packard, V. 1959. *The Status Seekers.* David McKay, New York.

Pappworth, M. H. 1969. *Human Guinea Pigs.* Penguin, Middlesex.

Papson, S. 1986. From symbolic exchange to bureaucratic discourse: the Hallmark greeting card. *Theory, Culture and Society.* 3(2): 99–111.

Paré, A. 1982 (1573). *On Monsters and Marvels.* Translated J. Pallister. University of Chicago Press, Chicago.

Parkin, M. 1989. Molly's face: the facts. *London Telegraph Weekend Magazine.* 18 February, 38–40.

Parsons, C., T. Iacono and L. Rozner 1987. Tongue reduction and articulation in children with Down Syndrome. *Australian Journal of Human Communication Disorders.* 15(2): 3–13.

Payne, B. 1965. *A History of Costume.* Harper and Row, New York.

Penry, J. 1936. *Character From The Face.* Hutchinson and Co., London.

Pickering, P. P., J. E. Williams, T. R. Vecchione 1980. Augmentation mammaplasty. In Goldwyn 1980. 696–706.

Poe, E. A. 1847 (1981). *Tales of the Grotesque.* Doubleday, New York.

Poggioli, R. 1968. *The Theory of the Avant-Garde.* Belknap Press, Harvard University Press, Cambridge, Mass.

Pouchelle, M-C. 1990. *The Body and Surgery in the Middle Ages.* Polity, Cambridge.

Rees, T. 1973a. Blepharoplasty. In T. Rees and D. Wood-Smith 1973. 44–133.

Rees, T. 1973b. The face lift. In T. Rees and D. Wood-Smith 1973. 134–212.

Rees, T. and D. Wood-Smith (eds) 1973. *Cosmetic Facial Surgery.* W. B. Saunders Co., Philadelphia.

Bibliography

Régnier-Bohler, D. 1988. Imagining the self. In Duby 1988a. 311–93.

Ribeiro, A. 1987. *The Female Face*. The Tate Gallery, London.

Rice, S. 1988. *Some Doctors Make You Sick*. Angus and Robertson, Sydney.

Richardson, S. 1971. Handicap, appearance and stigma. *Social Science and Medicine*. 5, 621–8.

Rinaldo, P. 1986. *Oriental Blondes*. (Documentary film) SVT, Sweden.

Roach, M. E. and J. Eichler 1973. *The Visible Self: Perspectives on Dress*. Prentice-Hall, New Jersey.

Roach, M. E. and J. Eichler (eds) 1979. *The Fabrics of Culture*. Mouton, The Hague.

Roberts, H. 1977. The exquisite slave: the role of clothes in the making of the Victorian woman. *Signs*. 2(3): 554–69.

Rosaldo, L. 1984. Toward an anthropology of self-feeling. In R. Shweder and R. LeVine (eds) *Culture Theory*. Cambridge University Press, Cambridge.

Roth, H. and R. Comie 1968. *The Little People*. Everest House, New York.

Rubbo, M. 1983. *Daisy: The Story of a Face Lift*. National Film Board of Canada.

Russo, M. 1986. Female grotesques: carnival and theory. In T. de Lauretis (ed.) *Feminist Studies Critical Studies*. Indiana University Press, Bloomington. 213–29.

Schacht, P. and A. Pemberton 1985. What is unnecessary surgery? Who shall decide? Issues of consumer sovereignty, conflict and self-regulation. *Social Science and Medicine*. 20(3): 199–206.

Scott, R. 1981. *The Body as Property*. Allen Lane, London.

'Secreta Secretorum' (extracts in English). 15th cent. British Library, Sloane MS 213, ff. 118v–119.

Serpell, J. 1986. *In The Company of Animals*. Blackwell, Oxford.

Sennett, R. 1976. *The Fall of Public Man*. Cambridge University Press, Cambridge.

Shapin, S. 1975. Phrenological knowledge and the social structure of early nineteenth century Edinburgh. *Annals of Science*. 32, 219–43.

Shapin, S. 1979. Homo phrenologicus: anthropological perspectives on an historical problem. In B. Barnes and S. Shapin (eds) *Natural Order: Historical Studies of Scientific Culture*. Sage London.

Shapiro, S. 1987. Sex, gender and fashion in medieval and early modern Britain. *Journal of Popular Culture*. 20(4): 113–28.

Bibliography

Sharpe, W. D. 1964. *Isidore of Seville: The Medical Writings*. American Philosophical Society, Philadelphia.

Shelley, M. 1818 (1967). *Frankenstein or The Modern Prometheus*. Bantam Books, New York.

Showalter, E. 1983. Critical cross-dressing: male feminists and the woman of the year. *Raritan*. 3(2): 130–49.

Simmel, G. 1904 (1971). Fashion. In Simmel 1971. 294–323.

Simmel, G. 1950. Adornment. In *The Sociology of Georg Simmel*. Free Press, New York. 338–44.

Simmel, G. 1971. *On Individuality and Social Forms*. University of Chicago Press, Chicago.

Simmel, G. 1980. *The Philosophy of Money*. Routledge and Kegan Paul, London.

Simmel, G. 1984. *On Women, Sexuality and Love*. Yale University Press, New Haven and London.

Snyder, G. 1974. Planning an augmentation mammaplasty. *Plastic and Reconstructive Surgery*. 54, 132–41.

Solomon, M. (ed.) 1985. *The Psychology of Fashion*. Lexington Books, D. C. Heath and Co, Mass.

Solow, C. 1977. Psycho-social aspects of intestinal by-pass surgery for massive obesity: current status. *American Journal of Clinical Nutrition*. 30, 103–8.

Sontag, S. 1966. *Against Interpretation*. Dell, New York.

Sontag, S. 1977. *Illness As Metaphor*. Farrar, Straus and Giroux, New York.

Sontag, S. 1980. *Under the Sign of Saturn*. Vintage, New York.

Sontag, S. 1989. *AIDS and Its Metaphors*. Farrar, Straus and Giroux, New York.

Spicker, S. F. 1976. Terra firma and infirma species: from medical philosophical anthropology to philosophy of medicine. *Journal of Medicine and Philosophy*. 1(2): 104–35.

Spira, M., F. J. Gerow and S. B. Hardy 1974. Complications of chemical face peeling. *Plastic and Reconstructive Surgery*. 54, 397–403.

Spon, J. 1934. *Faces: What They Mean and How To Read Them*. E. & F. N. Spon Ltd., London.

Stanworth, M. (ed.) 1987. *Reproductive Technologies*. Polity, Cambridge.

Steele, V. 1985. *Fashion and Eroticism*. Oxford University Press, New York.

Steiner, G. 1981. The archives of Eden. *Salmagundi*. 50–1: 57–89.

Bibliography

Stevenson, R. L. 1886 (1979). *Dr Jekyll and Mr Hyde*. Penguin, Middlesex.

Stewart, A. L. and R. H. Brook 1983. Effects of being overweight. *American Journal of Public Health*. 73, 171–8.

Stockholder, F. 1987. Mirrors and narcissism. *Theory, Culture and Society*. 4(1): 107–23.

Stone, G. 1962. Appearance and the self. In A. Rose (ed.) *Human Behavior and Social Processes*. Houghton Mifflin, Boston. 86–118.

Storr, A. 1988. *Solitude: A Return to the Self*. Free Press, New York.

Taylor, R. 1979. *Medicine Out of Control*. Sun Books, Melbourne.

Thompson, C. J. S. 1930. *The Mystery and Lore of Monsters*. Williams and Norgate, London.

Trilling, L. 1972. *Sincerity and Authenticity*. Harvard University Press, Cambridge, Mass.

Truzzi, M. 1968. Lilliputians in Gulliver's land: the social role of the dwarf. In M. Truzzi (ed.) *Sociology of Everyday Life*. Prentice-Hall, New Jersey. 13–27.

Turner, B. S. 1984. *The Body and Society: Explorations in Social Theory*. Blackwell, Oxford.

Turner, G. 1641. 'A Collection taken out of many Authors for my owne private use not onely of Astronomie but allso of Natureall and Artificiall Astrologie with other verie good rules and observationes.' British Library, Sloane MS 3570.

Turner, R. H. 1976. The true self: from institution to impulse. *American Journal of Sociology*. 81, 989–1007.

Tytler, G. 1982. *Physiognomy in the European Novel. Faces and Fortunes*. Princeton University Press, New Jersey.

Veblen, T. 1899. *The Theory of the Leisure Class*. Macmillan, New York.

Vico, G. 1744 (1968). *The New Science of Giambattista Vico*. Cornell University Press, New York. Translated by T. G. Bergin and M. H. Fisch.

von Boehn, M. 1932. *Modes and Manners*. 5 vols Benjamin Blom, New York.

Waddington, I. 1973. The role of the hospital in the development of modern medicine: a sociological analysis. *Sociology*. 7, 210–24.

Walker, J. H., M. Thomas and J. T. Russell 1971. Spina bifida and the parents. *Developmental Medicine and Child Neurology*. 13, 462–76.

Warkany, J. 1959. Congenital malformations in the past. *Journal of Chronic Diseases*. 10(2): 84–96.

Bibliography

Watson, W. 1749. Some accounts of the fetus in utero being differently affected by the smallpox. *Philosophical Transactions of the
Royal Society*. 46, 235–40.

Watson, J. 1980. Breast augmentation by use of dermal-fat grafts. In
Goldwyn 1980. 950–5.

Watts, G. T. 1982. Reconstructive surgery of the breast. In P. G.
Bevan (ed.) *Reconstructive Procedures in Surgery*. Blackwell Scientific Publications, Oxford. 409–29.

Webster, G. 1980. Cosmetic rhinoplasty. In Goldwyn 1980. 548–56.

Wells, S. 1867. *New Physiognomy, or, Signs of Character*. Fowler and
Wells, New York.

Weschler, J. 1982. *The Human Comedy: Physiognomy and Carica-
ture in 19th Century Paris*. University of Chicago Press, Chicago.

West, N. 1957. Miss Lonelyhearts. In *The Complete Works*. Farrar,
Straus and Giroux, New York.

Whiteside, R. L. 1974. *Face Language*. Frederick Fell Publishers,
New York.

Wilde, O. 1966. The Picture of Dorian Gray. In V. Holland (ed.)
Complete Works. Vol. 1. Collins, London. 17–167.

Williams, Raymond 1980. *Problems in Materialism and Culture*. Ver-
so, London.

Williams, Rosalind 1982. *Dream Worlds: Mass Consumption in Late
Nineteenth-Century France*. University of California Press, Berkeley.

Williamson, J. 1983. *Decoding Advertisements*. Marion Boyars, London.

Wilson, E. 1985. *Adorned In Dreams*. Virago, London.

Wittgenstein, L. 1967. *Philosophical Investigations*. Blackwell, Oxford.

Wooley, S. and O. Wooley 1979. Obesity and women Part 1.
Women's Studies International Quarterly. 2(1): 69–80.

Wooley, O., S. Wooley and S. Dyrenforth 1979. Obesity and women
Part 2. *Women's Studies International Quarterly*. 2(1): 81–92.

Wooley, O. W. and S. 1982. The Beverly Hills eating disorder: the
mass marketing of anorexia nervosa. *International Journal of
Eating Disorders*. 1(3): 57–69.

Wrobel, A. (ed.) 1988. *Pseudo-science and Society in Nineteenth-
Century America*. University Press of Kentucky, Lexington.

Zola, E. 1883 (1957). *Ladies' Delight*. John Calder, London.

Index